EARLY AUTUMN FOLIAGE AT OKEFENOKEE SWAMP PARK

A CARPET OF WATER LILIES EDGING A CYPRESS ISLAND

AFTERNOON LIGHT ACROSS A MARSH

CYPRESSES MIRRORED IN THE MIDDLE FORK RUN

YELLOW-FLOWERED TICKSEED IN MIST

A PAIR OF CAVORTING ANHINGAS

SUNSET BEHIND A DENSE SWAMP FOREST

TIME
LIFE
BOOKS ®

Other Publications:

HEALTHY HOME COOKING
UNDERSTANDING COMPUTERS
YOUR HOME
THE ENCHANTED WORLD
THE KODAK LIBRARY OF CREATIVE PHOTOGRAPHY
GREAT MEALS IN MINUTES
THE CIVIL WAR
PLANET EARTH
COLLECTOR'S LIBRARY OF THE CIVIL WAR
THE EPIC OF FLIGHT
THE GOOD COOK
WORLD WAR II
HOME REPAIR AND IMPROVEMENT
THE OLD WEST

For information on and a full description of any
of the Time-Life Books series listed above,
please write:

    Reader Information
    Time-Life Books
    541 North Fairbanks Court
    Chicago, Illinois 60611

Time-Life Books Inc. offers a wide range of fine
recordings, including a *Big Bands* series. For
subscription information, call 1-800-621-7026,
or write TIME-LIFE MUSIC, Time & Life
Building, Chicago, Illinois 60611.

This volume is one of a series that explores the
wild regions of the United States, the
Caribbean, Mexico and Central America.

THE OKEFENOKEE SWAMP

THE AMERICAN WILDERNESS/TIME-LIFE BOOKS/ALEXANDRIA, VIRGINIA

BY FRANKLIN RUSSELL
AND THE EDITORS OF TIME-LIFE BOOKS

WITH PHOTOGRAPHS BY PATRICIA CAULFIELD

Time-Life Books Inc.
is a wholly owned subsidiary of

TIME INCORPORATED

FOUNDER: Henry R. Luce 1898-1967

Editor-in-Chief: Henry Anatole Grunwald
President: J. Richard Munro
Chairman of the Board: Ralph P. Davidson
Corporate Editor: Ray Cave
Group Vice President, Books: Reginald K. Brack Jr.
Vice President, Books: George Artandi

TIME-LIFE BOOKS INC.
EDITOR: George Constable
Director of Design: Louis Klein
Director of Editorial Resources: Phyllis K. Wise
Acting Text Director: Ellen Phillips
Editorial Board: Russell B. Adams Jr., Dale M. Brown,
Roberta Conlan, Thomas H. Flaherty, Donia Ann Steele,
Rosalind Stubenberg, Kit van Tulleken, Henry Woodhead
Director of Research and Photography: John Conrad Weiser

PRESIDENT: Reginald K. Brack Jr.
Executive Vice Presidents: John M. Fahey Jr.,
Christopher T. Linen
Senior Vice Presidents: James L. Mercer,
Leopoldo Toralballa
Vice Presidents: Stephen L. Bair, Ralph J. Cuomo, Juanita T.
James, Hallett Johnson III, Robert H. Smith, Paul R. Stewart
Director of Production Services: Robert J. Passantino

THE AMERICAN WILDERNESS
Editorial Staff for The Okefenokee Swamp:
EDITOR: Charles Osborne
Designer: Charles Mikolaycak
Staff Writers: Simone D. Grossner, Anne Horan,
Gerald Simons
Chief Researcher: Martha T. Goolrick
Researchers: Joan Chambers, Rhea Finkelstein,
Beatrice Hsia, Myra Mangan
Copy Coordinators: Barbara Quarmby, Heidi Sanford
Design Assistant: Vincent Lewis
Picture Coordinator: Joan Lynch

Revisions Staff
EDITOR: Rosalind Stubenberg
Chief Researcher: Barbara Levitt
Text Editor: Sarah Brash
Art Assistant: Jeanne Potter
Copy Coordinator: Cynthia Kleinfeld
Editorial Assistants: Mary Kosak, Linda Yates

Editorial Operations
Copy Chief: Diane Ullius
Editorial Operations: Caroline A. Boubin (manager)
Production: Celia Beattie
Quality Control: James J. Cox (director)
Library: Louise D. Forstall

The Author: Franklin Russell, a native of New Zealand who now lives in New Jersey, is a journalist and musician as well as a naturalist. He has written numerous books based on his studies of wilderness areas, including *Watchers at the Pond, Argen the Gull, The Secret Islands, Wild Creatures* and *Searchers at the Gulf.* He is also the author of a number of children's books.

The Cover: A watercourse deep inside the Okefenokee reflects a stand of cypresses draped with Spanish moss. The stillness of the water, the stately trees and the single bloom of a fragrant water lily combine to capture the essence of the swamp.

The Photographer: Patricia Caulfield began her study of photography at George Eastman House during her undergraduate years at the University of Rochester. After graduating in 1953, she joined the editorial staff of *Modern Photography* and was the magazine's executive editor when she left in 1967 to concentrate on nature photography and the field of conservation. Her pictures have frequently appeared in *Audubon* and *Natural History* magazines, and she is the photographer-producer of *Everglades,* a Sierra Club book.

CORRESPONDENTS: Elisabeth Kraemer-Singh (Bonn); Dorothy Bacon (London); Maria Vincenza Aloisi (Paris); Ann Natanson (Rome). Valuable assistance was also provided by: Judy Aspinall, Karin B. Pearce (London); Ruth Annan (Miami); Carolyn T. Chubet, Miriam Hsia, Christina Lieberman (New York); Mimi Murphy (Rome).

Library of Congress Cataloguing in Publication Data
Russell, Franklin, 1922-
The Okefenokee Swamp.
(The American wilderness)
Bibliography: p. 180.
Includes index.
1. Natural history—Okefenokee Swamp.
2. Swamp ecology—Okefenokee Swamp.
3. Okefenokee Swamp
I. Time-Life Books. II. Title.
QH105.G4R87   574.5'2632   73-87582
ISBN 0-8094-1200-4
ISBN 0-8094-1202-0 lib. bdg.
ISBN 0-8094-1201-2 retail ed.

TIME-LIFE is a trademark of Time Incorporated U.S.A.

Contents

A Small, Enchanted Corner of the Old South

Compared with other United States wildernesses, the Okefenokee Swamp is a small place, covering 685 square miles mainly in southeastern Georgia, with a slight overlap into Florida (blue spot, above). It is a fascinating realm that both confirms and contradicts popular notions of a swamp (patterned green area on map at left). Along with stately cypresses, peat quagmires and dim waterways, the Okefenokee has sandy pine islands, sunlit prairies and clear lakes.

Originally formed in a shallow depression scooped out by the Atlantic Ocean (supplementary map, page 22), the swamp drains mostly to the southwest, by way of the Suwannee River, into the Gulf of Mexico, though some of its sluggish waters flow via the St. Marys River to the Atlantic.

Only three roads lead into the swamp, going to Okefenokee Swamp Park, Suwannee Canal Recreation Area and Stephen Foster State Park, but several small-boat trails (blue dotted lines) thread the interior. All but 55 square miles of the swamp belong to the Okefenokee National Wildlife Refuge, which, along with state parks as well as a privately owned area, is outlined in red.

1/ Among the Trembling Trees

This unbelievable realm of mystery and charm . . . is as fantastic as a page from Arabian Nights, but as real as Nature itself.   LISTON ELKINS/ STORY OF THE OKEFENOKEE

When the alligators bellowed shortly after midnight I awoke startled, for a moment thinking I was in Africa again with lions near the camp. The bellowing seemed far off, yet also close, loud and muted at the same time. I lay there for a long moment, drowsy and uncertain, then realized I had awakened in a tent at the edge of the Okefenokee Swamp. I was hearing the last great primeval voice of the North American continent. Such was the brutal, thrilling power of the sound that the hair on the back of my neck stiffened.

The voice of the alligator is the best introduction that any newcomer can have to this natural wonder of the continent, an American wilderness some 680 square miles in extent, within easy reach of the well-traveled Atlantic coast. The alligator's voice is not merely a primeval one speaking from the wilderness. It is a reminder to modern man that the quality of his civilization is so far removed from this wilderness that he may understand it only with much difficulty.

Listening to the alligators as a naturalist, I could conjure up the memory of thousands of great beasts being killed to make shoes or handbags or wallets when the resources of America were considered inexhaustible and when nobody cared whether a single alligator was left to roar in its swamp or not. Listening as a historian, I was glad the alligators were still out there, surviving triumphantly, while a parade of different sorts of men—Creek, Seminole, Army deserters, black refugees, lumbermen, turpentiners, farmers, fishermen and hunters—had come and gone from the swamp, and there was hardly an echo of their voices. But my most satisfying thought as I lay in the lightening gloom of the tent was that some of America's most experienced engineers, most audacious entrepreneurs, most rapacious exploiters, men who had spent nearly a century trying to wreck the swamp or turn it into farmland, had also come and gone. The swamp and its growling thunder of voices were still there.

I had another thought, this one less explicable. Although I had not yet really entered the swamp, had not seen a cypress tree close up, or an alligator out of a zoo, the Okefenokee had somehow reached out already and touched me. For years I had wandered around the world alone in many wildernesses of tundra, icecap, barrens, mountain range, desert and open ocean, and had always had a special fondness for being alone, at least temporarily, as far from civilization as possible.

But here, in a tent not more than half a mile from a tourist camp, hotdog stands, soda machines and air-conditioned trailers, I felt an unaccustomed expectation. There was something in the quality of those alligator voices that shattered orderly civilized thinking and replaced it with a fierce atavistic pleasure. Ahead of me lay a special experience: penetrating a unique world.

Long before coming to the swamp I had read something of its contradictions. It is North American, surrounded by the works of man, yet it is as wild as anything in Central America or Africa. To many people a swamp connotes mud; but there is relatively little mud in the Okefenokee. Instead, it is filled with peat overlying a layer of sand that ranges from two to 15 feet in thickness. The sand was once the bed of the Atlantic Ocean, when its waters covered what is now southern Georgia. Ocean currents and surf action gradually built up an offshore sandbar, and between it and the shore a depression formed. This ancient depression is the site of the modern Okefenokee. The sandbar survives as Trail Ridge, a 40-mile-long crest at the swamp's eastern edge.

The Okefenokee Swamp is actually an immense, slow-running body of water with congregations of tall cypresses, vast areas of sphagnum moss, dense thickets of shrubs and islands thronged with pines. From its northernmost reaches in Georgia, about 40 miles north of the Florida border (map, pages 18-19), the swamp flows south some 20 miles until the moving water reaches roughly the midpoint of the Okefenokee. There, approximately at a large island, Billy's, a branch turns westward and heads for the Suwannee River exit into the Gulf of Mexico.

Meanwhile, at a point about 15 miles southwest of Billy's Island, another branch begins to flow out through a stream that becomes the St. Marys River. This river exits into the Atlantic Ocean north of the city of Jacksonville.

The Okefenokee is reputed to be gloomy and forbidding, a place of mystery and terror, yet I knew already it was a world of millions of singing creatures—insects, reptiles, amphibians, birds—and a 438,610-acre garden of spectacular flower displays. It was a wilderness, yet a wilderness that had been well trodden by impatient man. It had sheltered Indians so sophisticated in their way of life that their origins were long a mystery, and then white men who became unique creatures under the swamp's spell. It was a wilderness but it had once contained a bustling town built in its heartland. It had been an odd battleground between animal, plant and man, but the animals and plants had eventually prevailed and the men had become educated to understand some part of the meaning of the wilderness.

Before entering the swamp I had flown over it and had looked down on absolutely trackless country. From the air, the swamp is not neatly divided into prairie, bog and island. The prairies are so well overgrown with water plants that, in midsummer, little open water shows anywhere. The islands seem not to be distinguishable at all. The pines do not always stop at their sandy shores, but melt into cypress and bay trees and shrubs in territory that is part water, part peat, part sand. It is a daunting sight, with wilderness stretching out of view in all directions. The distances even when viewed from a comfortable seat in a plane are enough to make the legs go weak.

Two thirds down the Okefenokee's eastern border, which adjoins Georgia's coastal plain, the swamp has been visibly breached by man. From the air the scene presents a striking resemblance to the outlines of ancient canals in the dry Mesopotamian floodplain. A man-built canal, monument to all wilderness destroyers, cuts as direct as a Roman road through the crazy-quilt pattern of islands and meandering lakes and prairies. It looks as though it had been built yesterday instead of over 75 years ago.

And now I was on the ground, at the edge of the swamp in early spring, ready to make a series of expeditions into it, to follow the tracks of both animal and man, and to bring out a subjective impression of the Okefenokee as a place. What had caught my imagination long before I entered the swamp was how long it had preserved its primeval en-

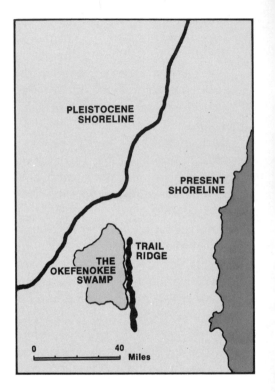

The Okefenokee began to take shape more than 250,000 years ago, when the shoreline of the Atlantic lay some 75 miles inland from the present Georgia coast. Between the shore and a narrow sandbar (Trail Ridge) a shallow basin formed. After the ocean had receded, the basin filled with fresh water as a warming climate melted the last Ice Age glaciers about 7,000 years ago and caused the water table to rise. Impermeable clay beneath the swamp keeps it from draining.

vironment. The last Florida wolf known to have been killed there was dispatched in 1910. The rare ivory-billed woodpecker found one of its last refuges there. The cougar may still hang on in there, a survivor of man's invasion—his lumbering, his harvesting of thousands of gallons of turpentine, his hunting with dogs and guns.

The swamp compressed into one almost self-contained world a diversity of wildlife made unique by the strangeness of the environment. It was a place where black bears could flourish and become quarter-ton monsters, where marsh rabbits swam like ducks, then darted across quaking bogs as lightly as thistledown in the wind, where 10 billion bees made matchless honey from acres of floating flowers, where teeming cities of water birds were sheltered.

The swamp had been well measured long before I got there, its creatures listed, its places described, its geography traversed. But I had come to make my own appraisal, to examine this place with my head filled by 30 years of watching wildernesses everywhere being ripped to pieces or blown up or flattened or paved over. I could not spend a lifetime in the Okefenokee as many people had done before me, exploiting and enjoying, quantifying and qualifying the place; but I could perhaps measure its essence. Was there, in fact, any meaning to this wilderness? Did we need it? More specifically, did I need it?

All I knew for sure was that other people before me had felt its odd drawing power, people who had not been into the swamp either. It had affected William Bartram, a naturalist who had voyaged near it in the spring of 1773. He knew he was passing one of the world's wonders, knew that he should try to explore it but did not, or could not. Yet in his 1791 book, *Travels*, Bartram's description of the Okefenokee, garnered from talks with local Creek, was highly colored, even accounting for the hyperbole of 18th Century travel literature. There was a terrestrial paradise, Bartram reported, where gorgeous women (so beautiful they were called daughters of the sun) rescued lost Creek and fed them oranges, dates and corn cakes while warning them that their husbands were so fierce and cruel no intruder could enter the swamp and survive for long.

The swamp remained inscrutable into the next century, yet writers continued to describe it with detailed confidence. Another traveler, Paul Fountain, in his *Great Deserts and Forests of North America*, gave it 23 pages, including the note that "the Okefinoke has not, I think, been often penetrated; it certainly had not at the time I visited it in 1871 and 1876." Later travelers suspected that he probably never reached the swamp at all. Even the name of the place remained elusive. No white man could hope to grasp the intricacies of the Indian pronunciation of the word—which means shaking earth. The modern name has a vague resemblance to the original Indian sound, but an old Georgia map of 1790 recorded it as *Ekanfinaka,* which, on another map 20 years later, had become *Eckenfinooka.* It was not until nearly 100 years after William Bartram's voyage that maps began producing a name recognizable by modern standards—*Okefinoke.* The pronunciation then—*Oak-fin-oak*—is still used by some locals today, but most people prefer the more musical *Oakee-fen-oakee.*

This elusiveness of identity, I knew, was shared by the Suwannee River, which is inseparable from the swamp because it drains most of the Okefenokee into the Gulf of Mexico. The Suwannee was, and is, a water highway replete with its own myths. A legendary Ethiopian, King Nero, is said to have once led refugee slaves along its banks to new, free lives. This was the water road, according to another myth, that had brought the Maya from Yucatán into the swamp centuries ago to become its first shadowy people. They gave the river the name Water Beloved of the Sun God, which seems vaguely consonant with the "daughters of the sun" later mentioned by Bartram. But the Seminole dismissed the sun-god myth and said the river was named for a chieftainess, Su-Wan-Nee. The Spaniards agreed with neither the Maya nor the Seminole and insisted that the river was the Little St. Johns River, and that Suwannee was a corruption of San Juanito.

Swamp and river thus maintain their community of mystery. It is possible to describe the Okefenokee as a "peat-filled bog" straddling the Georgia-Florida border near the Atlantic coast, as one official brochure does, and this is both accurate and untrue because it reduces the swamp to an unpleasant image of immense dreariness. It is possible to count its islands, about 70, and to say that they cover 25,000 acres, and this is also true, but it says nothing of their having been the sites of bitter battles between dogs and bears and cougars, of their having sprouted crops of corn and vegetables and great whispering plantations of slash pines surrounded by the stark grandeur of water-loving cypresses.

It is possible to talk about 60,000 acres of prairies, the flooded open areas choked with water lilies and neverwets, pipeworts and ferns, with maiden canes and sedges and moss, but this is only one facet of the great swamp. It is possible to describe the hammocks, those dense labyrinths of twisted growth, odd collections of hardwoods, water oaks, live oaks and magnolias, clustered together, but parts of the Everglades, hundreds of miles to the south, have bigger and better hammocks.

Before reaching the edge of the swamp, I had decided to enter it alone. This was against all advice and contrary to the orders of the guardians of the swamp. Part of the northern fringe of the swamp is owned by a private corporation, the Okefenokee Swamp Park, set up by the citizens of Waycross, Georgia, the nearest town. There tourists get guided tours of the northern swamp that start from park headquarters on Cowhouse Island. From the federal government, the state of Georgia leases one small part of the swamp, administered as Stephen Foster State Park, a long projection of land that enters the swamp from the southwest, near the banks of the outgoing Suwannee River. There, too, is a tourist information center and boat-tour entrance point. Most of the rest of the swamp is a federal tract called the Okefenokee National Wildlife Refuge (including 353,980 acres of National Wilderness Area), which has its official entrance in the southeastern fringes of the swamp at a tourist center called the Suwannee Canal Recreation Area.

Each of these swamp guardians shares a common understanding of the dangers of the primeval swamp and demands, correctly, that anyone who wants to wander in the swamp alone must be out by nightfall, although federal officials may give canoeists and organized campers a special permit to remain in the Okefenokee overnight. Everywhere that it is safe to travel, marked boat trails guide tourists through the trackless wastes. When travelers get lost, which happens occasionally, airplanes and airboats locate them quickly.

Still, it is against common sense to wander around the swamp alone. For one thing, its waters are in constant flux, high one week, abruptly lower the next. A watercourse may suddenly be obstructed when a mass of once-submerged peat is forced upward by gases that are the product of underwater vegetative decay. The swamp traveler may also be stranded if his craft is damaged, or worse he may run afoul of an alligator or a rattler or a coral snake.

I decided to go into the swamp by myself, though my intention was not to incur senseless danger. It is impossible to know a mountain by ripping over it in a snowmobile or to understand a desert from the seat of a roaring trail bike. I did not want to be encumbered by either the chatter of a guide or the sound of an outboard motor. I wanted to move into the swamp and become a part of its own magisterial pace, and for that I was prepared to take some degree of risk.

The day would soon be dawning and it was time to move.

But to take that secret step out of civilization was almost as difficult as it had been in centuries past. To reach my canoe, hidden in bushes on the northeastern fringe of the swamp, meant a long walk through pines, then through mossy bogland studded with shrubs until I reached water. Old swamp men used to say that to understand the Okefenokee you had to walk it, and this was the most exhausting travel known to man. "Sometimes it would seem to hardened veterans like us," said a determined swamp botanist in the 1920s, "that we could not pull another leg out for a step forward. We might sink to knee or waist."

In the gloom I misjudged the solid ground on the way to the canoe and instead walked onto what seemed to be firm greensward. This was a stretch of the famous trembling earth—loose, wet peat from which grew a clotted mixture of grasses and water plants and young cypresses with small pliable roots, yet so close together that they looked like solid earth. For a hundred steps this held me up, the small trees shaking around me, as long as I kept moving and got one foot out of the muck before it sank too deep.

But it was not until later, elsewhere in the swamp, that I really understood what was meant by "trembling earth." The peat and vegetation were more thickly compacted, and bore my weight, but because the mass was flexible, it felt something like a water bed. As I walked across it, the growth beneath my feet received the shock and transmitted it back, causing a sensation of trembling.

Now the sun rose, a glaring pink eye showing through pines behind me, and shone on a rather desperate traveler who was beginning to doubt that he would ever find his boat. But at least, in this softer stuff, I could wade. The muck became thinner and eventually I trod a harder bottom and so reached the canoe.

The alligators had generally become silent and the swamp now sounded with the sharp interrogative cries of birds; hidden sparrows nearby, water birds somewhere in the distance. Spread before me was a variegation of patches of open water, clots of floating plants, thickets of holly and other shrubs, the scene unfolding to its inevitable climax of gaunt cypresses lining my limited horizon. Egrets flew overhead as I paddled through the undergrowth along a water roadway probably pioneered by an alligator. Water flowed almost imperceptibly along it. There is hardly any stagnant water in the swamp. The movement of water to the southwest creates the tempo of the swamp. It slows down the human traveler as well.

A shallow feeder creek, its coffee color derived from acids released by decaying vegetation, flows slowly toward the Suwannee River.

Shrubs closed in on the canoe and scraped its sides with brittle branches, a mélange of different species all roughly resembling one another—hollies, huckleberries and fetterbushes with vines interweaving. These vines are called black and red bamboos, and their harsh spines are formidable. The hollies' slender trunks thickened ahead of me and paraded a blotching of red lichens. The hollies yielded to cypresses, graceful and silent. I began to get the first real feeling of the swamp. It is one of subtlety, of delicate shades of green and brown and gray, of diaphanous decorations of Spanish moss, shimmering reflections, solitary flowers touching yellow wood, a silent woodpecker clamped to a branch, a heron standing rigidly still in imitation of a plant. The cypresses created an illusion of my being inside something, some natural edifice where the order of things was dominated by the guardianship of these great trees. It was a very odd feeling, a bit uncomfortable at first, and I paddled forward quickly.

The cypresses fell behind and a prairie appeared ahead, studded with stunted cypresses. These open areas are called prairies because, when the teeming aquatic plants have closed in on a swamp lake, they transform it into what appears to be a kind of rough grassland. Some of these, like carex, pack together and look like parts of the sawgrass meadows of the Everglades. Others, like the maiden canes, gather densely at the fringes of more solid patches of bog. Common water lilies abound wherever they can float, while in the dark water itself an inconceivably dense and persistent branching of brown growth of bladderworts is visible almost everywhere. Buzzing dragonflies surrounded the canoe or settled on floating leaves, each of these creatures dressed in a different color.

The prairies not only teem with plants; they are hunting grounds. Here, I knew, when alligators lay dormant in midwinter chill, Indian and white hunters had tracked them to their deaths, following their long, winding, muddy trails. The canoe moved among a score of katydids that settled on the water surface. Then, to my astonishment, they all dived and disappeared. A delicate white flower, the floating heart, appeared by my paddle, apparently sitting on the pad of a lily. A tiny chorus frog, scarcely an inch long and almost invisible in the shadow of some long grasses, blew up its great neck sac almost as big as its own body and made a single trilling cry.

The prairie gave way to a belt of cypresses and then the water opened out in a lake—a long narrow finger moving among the cypresses, their images perfectly inverted in the still water. Random touches of color showed as warblers moved in dark places. This was more somber country. Most of the swamp lakes run more or less north and south, responding to the flow of water. I could see hundreds of tiny fish teeming in groups as I peered into the dark brown water. These were the beginnings of a cornucopia of fish populations—gars and suckers, perch and sunfish, bullheads and bluegills, bass and bowfin, silversides and darters. The fish, in turn, along with an almost equally diverse collection of turtles, were alligator food.

As the cypresses thickened and the air became gloomy around me, I could imagine the silence broken by many sounds. The swamp people are practically extinct. One old man, who had lived in a house on stilts and referred to a woman by the Elizabethan term of "mistress," had died only a dozen years before. He and most of his people were gone, and the echoes of their hollering (the grand opera of the Okefenokee, outsiders called it) were faint in my imagination because, unlike the reality of the alligator voices, I had never heard them. The hollering was, I had read, a combination of deep and shrill shouts uttered at daybreak or sunset, and the sound was authoritatively said either to chill or enchant a first-time listener. It was easier to imagine a more sinister background noise, the baying of ghost packs of swamp hounds howling their way in pursuit of bear and cougar, fox and raccoon. But now, an absolute silence prevailed.

Because the swamp consists of so many contrasting environments —prairie, thicket, lake, island, bog, hammock, the solid stands of timber called cypress bays—it is constantly inconstant. The cypresses were now so thick they formed a jungle, dripping moisture. The sound of massively running waters reached among the roots of the trees all around me. Yet in front of me was an ancient gnarled stump that was so well blackened it must have been destroyed by fire. Here was an abrupt reminder that this cosmos was impermanent. The swamp was capable of catastrophic changes of mood.

In winter, the dry season, its water level sometimes drops several feet, making boat travel almost impossible. Then the grasses dry out and water vegetation rots and perhaps fire starts. The Okefenokee has been almost completely burned over at least once in the last 200 years, a disaster that is difficult to visualize in a world so thoroughly dominated by water.

This was also hurricane country. Although I paddled through silence I knew the swamp could be turned into a terror of wind and rain. One

19th Century storm flattened entire pine forests on some of the islands, tangling thousands of trees together in indescribable confusion. Not even the massive live oaks of the hammocks survived; they fell in disorder and sank into the waters that had sustained them.

Now the cypresses thinned and the waterway opened into a wider lake. Ahead lay an island. Like many of the Okefenokee islands it was not much more than a sandbar that had been colonized by slash pines over most of its length. It was a barren island, the pines thin, straggly, as opposed to other islands where hardwoods had taken hold. The island was a study in the subtlety of the swamp. It looked barren but I knew that in the warmer months to come it would host an abundance of plants, scores of species of grasses, sedges, rushes, shrubs, lilies, milkworts, meadow beauties, vines and trees, in a kaleidoscope of orange and yellow, pink, green and white.

Oddly, the slow pace of travel sped the day. Long before I was hungry it had become too late to turn back to the edge of the swamp. I had been led on by the shuttling changes of scenes. These shifts, from prairie to lake, from island to cypress forest, from solid ground to trembling earth, were all part of the swamp's constantly changing face. I already knew from talking to people familiar with the Okefenokee that no day was like any other day in the swamp, no March resembled any other March, or any other month, and no year was like any other year. I knew I could drift forward like this for years and continue to see an endlessly varied procession of spectacles.

The swamp was continually renewing itself, shuffling its ingredients into fresh forms, new orders. A traveler might see scores of snakes in an hour of travel: cottonmouths, rattlers, king snakes, greens, rainbows and coachwhips coiled in tree branches, dozing on logs, slipping through the shallows. But he might never see this many in another score of years. He might hear a dozen mockingbirds singing together on one island, a delight never to be repeated.

There were wild turkeys in the swamp, and if I were lucky, I might see kites flashing across prairies in flights so recklessly engineered they looked suicidal. I had yet to meet some of the swamp's familiar creatures: prothonotary warblers and submarine-like anhingas, giant alligator snapping turtles and frogs smaller than a penny. I had yet to see female turtles bulldozing earth banks to make their nests or witness thrashing flights of ibises bolting upward against red sunsets. Awaiting me were parades of bluebirds and bobwhites, mockingbirds, catbirds, kingfishers, woodpeckers, all to be capped by great clouds of ducks swooping down out of autumn skies: mallards and ringnecks, black ducks and mergansers.

By this time, I was exhausted, temporarily surfeited. I drove the canoe ashore, the "shore" being nothing more than a thickening of grasses, the remains of a fallen log already rotting and half smothered with moss, a thicket of bushes half-circling my landing place. I overturned the canoe and sat on the log to watch the evening gather in the trees beyond my camping place. Almost immediately a powerful swirl broke the water a score of feet away and a fish leaped out and flopped down on a mass of lily leaves. Without thinking, I rushed into the water, grabbed the fish, and waded back.

It was a small pickerel. I had no fire but I slit it open, gutted it, chopped off the head and ate it raw. It was my imagination, of course, but nothing ever tasted better. A few frogs hailed the evening with clicks and grunts, moans and belches, and the sun left only the dark red stain of its disappearance behind the frieze of cypresses.

Just before I dozed off under the canoe, the night air suddenly burst wide open. I smashed my head against the canoe seat as I sat up in fright. The blast-furnace roar shook my heart into emergency pounding. Incredulous, I heard that awful sound repeated, but quieter, repeated again more distantly, echoed a third and fourth and fifth time in the fastnesses of the dark swamp.

Then I laughed. I had camped within a few feet of the Okefenokee's first spokesman for the evening. I laughed again and was laughing, half asleep, as the swelling thunder of alligator cries encircled me.

The Habitats of the Flowers

The traditional image of Southern swamps as dank and claustrophobic places is both true and untrue of the Okefenokee. Large parts of it answer this description, but other parts emphatically refute it. There are great open stretches where the horizon is low and unlimited. Clear lakes and ponds emerge from narrow, plant-clogged waterways. Far from being a monotony of green and brown, the Okefenokee flaunts an assortment of bright hues in some of the showiest wild flowers to be found in the Southeast. For every fading blossom, the bud of another plant opens, providing continuous bloom for nine months of the year.

Because of the length of the growing season the look of the Okefenokee is ever changing. But within its borders three kinds of major habitat are readily recognizable: prairies, moist pinelands and cypress bays. Each has its own character, in part dictated by the flowering plants that predominate. Of the three, the prairies are the most unexpected in appearance. Except in some grassy patches, they bear no resemblance to their Western namesakes. They are actually marshes, with a sandy bottom layered over by peat and covered with water to a depth sur-passed only in the swamp's main watercourses. Grasses, sedges and aquatic plants are the major vegetation, permitting wide, relatively treeless views under an open sky.

The moist pinelands are found on islands—the small sandbars left in the retreat of the sea that once covered the site of the Okefenokee. Only a few feet above the level of the surrounding swamp, they can easily be flooded by a good rain. They tend to be thick with trees —chiefly the moisture-loving slash pine—but they also have parklike clearings where sunlight pours in and promotes a luxuriant growth of shrubs and herbs that put on a show of the most spectacular blooms to be seen in the swamp.

The largest of the three habitats, and the most densely forested, has been staked out by the cypress trees. The most extensive of these areas —20 acres or more—are called bays, a misnomer perhaps borrowed from wooded swamps in Florida where bay trees flourish. Sunlight nourishes a dense flowering underbrush at the fringes of these cypress concentrations, but seldom reaches inside the bays. It is here that the swamp justifies its reputation as a place of deep, mysterious gloom.

Blooming rose pogonias, a species of wild orchid, compete for space in an Okefenokee prairie with budding pipeworts, a rushlike water plant also known as hatpin or bog button.

The Sprawling, Watery Prairies

Early settlers of the Okefenokee had their own terms for its varied settings, often using words that have very different meanings elsewhere. The word "prairie" is a striking example. To a Westerner it connotes large tracts of deep, fertile soil covered with tall, coarse grasses. For the swampers it described their marshes —low-lying regions usually covered by one to three feet of water and teeming with aquatic plant life—water lilies and golden clubs, tangles of redroot and pickerelweed, and stands of maiden cane. These areas may be small or large, ranging in extent from 40 acres to the more than 3,000 acres of Chase Prairie.

Scientists believe that Okefenokee prairies owe their existence to catastrophic drought followed by devastating fire—galloping conflagrations that destroyed whole stands of trees and their understory of shrubs—and slow-burning fires that burrowed deeply into the underlying peat, destroying the root systems of entrenched plants and carving out new depressions that served as catch basins when the waters returned. Prairies emerged out of the ashes and the new watery environment. In time they became home to a host of aquatic plants such as the half-dozen herbs shown in close-up at right. Still later, in the inexorable scheme of plant succession, trees secure a hold and multiply. The prairie's ultimate fate is to give way to the advancing forest.

REDROOT

GRASS PINK

Fringing waters dotted with lily pads, low-growi

PICKERELWEED

marsh grasses and pipeworts provide an unimpeded view across Chesser Prairie.

WATER LILY AND PADS

GOLDEN CLUB

PIPEWORT

ORANGE MILKWORT

MEADOW BEAUTY

Soaring above thickets of inkberry shrubs, a stand of pines occupies a former sandbar.

SWAMP MILKWEED

GERARDIA

DWARF LAUREL

INKBERRY

COLIC ROOT

The Preserves of the Pine

Solid ground in the Okefenokee is in short supply, accounting for only about 5 per cent of its total 436,600 acres. All of the solid ground takes the form of sandy islands; there are some 70 of them throughout the swamp that are 20 acres or more. Even these places do not guarantee a firm footing. Generally flat, barely elevated above the encircling swamp waters, they have little drainage and suffer frequent soakings.

The islands are the domain of the pine trees, particularly the fast-growing slash pine. Amid the stands of trees, sun-filled clearings—some created by controlled fires—encourage a diversity of plant growth unmatched anywhere in the swamp. Of the plants pictured at left, dwarf laurel and inkberry are but two of more than 70 species of shrubs found there, while the other plants shown represent an army of more than 300 species of herbs.

Wherever there are higher, drier spots on these islands—even if the elevation increases by no more than six to 12 inches—the longleaf pine, which favors dry soil, takes over from the slash pine. Sometimes dry soil meets moist soil and longleaf and slash pine coexist, as seen in the photograph at far left. A longleaf (foreground) rises from a rather bare patch of sand, while the slash pines at left and in the background have a luxuriant understory of inkberry, a member of the holly family that is found mostly in wetlands.

ST.-JOHN'S-WORT

Carpeted by purple bladderwort and flanked by climbing heath (left), the waters of

PURPLE TICKSEED

FETTERBUSH

pond clearing lap the edge of a cypress forest.

YELLOW MILKWORT

YELLOW-EYED GRASS

SWAMP HAW

The Sovereign Forests

About four fifths of the swamp is forest, in which the predominant tree is the cypress. It masses most spectacularly in the extensive stands known as bays, a distinctly soggy sort of habitat covered to a large extent with shallow water and dotted with numerous protruding tussocks of peat and humus.

It is in the interior of the bays, dim and brooding, that a visitor's preconceived notions about the look of the swamp are dramatically borne out. Walking becomes an exercise in slogging. Light and sun seldom filter in; only ferns and other shade-loving plants thrive, and no flowers bloom. But the story is different around the margins of the bays and in the relatively open areas of cypress ponds. In these places flowering shrubs and herbs, among them those shown at left, rival the plants of other Okefenokee habitats in their exuberant growth and color.

For the cypress, the bay provides an appropriate place to make its last majestic stand. At the same time the bay also serves as a rich source of seeds. Some remain and ultimately add to the density of the bay; some in time find their way to prairies *(overleaf)* to build a new outpost and begin the process of reforestation. The process is periodically held in check by the forces of fire and drought; otherwise, the persistently encroaching cypress would need only a few centuries to take over the entire Okefenokee.

A classic case of confrontation involving all three of the swamp's principal habitats appears at this edge of Chesser Prairie. While the

moist pinelands lining the horizon offer no threat of encroachment, the cypresses at right signal the initial thrust of an advancing forest.

2/ Echoes of the Dinosaurs

Reptiles are a part of the old wilderness of earth...in which man got the nerves and hormones that make him human. If we let the reptile go it is a sign we are ready to let all wilderness go.   ARCHIE CARR/ THE REPTILES

When I first went into the Okefenokee the physical presence of the alligator was a neutral force, a loglike form sculling itself across the bow of my canoe, a cold eye watching me from the unruffled stillness of a lake, a scaled body lying inert on the banks of an island, a torpedo shape gliding among the floating plants of a prairie. The creature seemed so somnolent, so static, and yet the more I traveled the more it impinged on my mind. Gradually it took on character in a series of vignettes I witnessed myself or heard described by others. There were supposed to be between 6,000 and 10,000 alligators in the swamp when I was there, a very low population compared with what the Okefenokee had once held, yet no part of it was empty of them. Their drag marks wound in and out of thickets, they crossed swampy stretches of islands and dug out long tunnels beneath the boggy muck, they hid in a turmoil of thrashed-up mud and swamp weed in their many holes or refuges. They were everywhere and anywhere.

The alligator perfectly sustains the primeval atmosphere of the Okefenokee. It comes of the same stock that produced the dinosaur; it is a living symbol of that great age, 200 million years ago, when dinosaurs and other reptiles dominated the earth. Like the slow-flowing water of the Okefenokee, the alligator's pace is leisurely, a tribute to a life span of half a century. Most of the time it is in no hurry to do anything. Now that practically all hunting for its hide has stopped, it is expanding in size without haste. The average length of an Okefenokee alligator seems to be around eight feet, although nobody knows what the maximum size might be. Nor does anyone know what—other than humans —ultimately kills the really big creatures. William Bartram claimed to have seen monsters of 20 feet or more and John James Audubon killed and measured one at 17 feet.

The alligator invites watching because it exemplifies a truth about the swamp: it is not what it seems. It appeared at first to be a motionless decoration, cold and remote; but that was because in the early spring I saw it only by day. The swamp, however, is a night place; that is its second truth. While by day the alligator is a half-sunken log, by night, like almost all the other animals there, it is transformed.

As spring advanced amid a flurry of winds and rains, the alligators surfaced at night in multitudes. My flashlight picked out a score of glistening disks, white and green—scales reflecting the beam. Alligators floated in almost every size, some no bigger than my hand, others almost as large as my canoe. They snapped up pig frogs, themselves just emerging from winter rest. They accelerated like torpedoes in pursuit of a frantically slithering snake or salamander. They rooted like pigs in mud for crayfish. Often, beyond the range of my light, the crash of jaws and the crunch of breaking bone and shell sounded. Alligators hunt and eat everything, occasionally their own kind, but turtles are special favorites and the night noise of their shells smashing is a footnote to primordial history. I saw one large alligator on Half Moon Lake with a turtle weighing perhaps 10 pounds between its jaws, the desperate head of the victim snaking back and forth. Then the alligator submerged, leaving only the captive turtle's head above water. It did not look like a good way to die.

Most of the alligator's world remains permanently beyond human vision, but some of it can be deduced from the night sounds. The slap of jaws and the squawking of fleeing birds tell a story. The water birds, herons, rails, gallinules and coots, walking across swamp vegetation, are never sure that a tiny disturbance in the weeds does not signify a small alligator lurking in ambush. I caught glimpses of these collisions of evolution—wary warm-bloods venturing into water owned by the cold-bloods. Muskrats and raccoons appeared briefly as tense statues in the moonlight, never knowing when their foraging for food in a pond was safe. Shallowness of water was no guarantee.

Nearly all early accounts of Okefenokee life tell of the aggressiveness of the alligators, how they sometimes attacked boats and bit chunks out of the sides, how they lunged at dogs and often killed them. When William Bartram sailed down the St. Johns, he noted that "The River . . . from shore to shore, and perhaps near half a mile above and below me, appeared to be one solid bank of fish . . . pushing through this narrow pass of St. Juan's into the little lake . . . the alligators were in such incredible numbers, and so close together from shore to shore, that it would have been easy to have walked across their heads, had the animals been harmless . . . whilst this mighty army of fish were forcing the pass . . . thousands, I may say hundreds of thousands, of them were caught and swallowed by the devouring alligators . . . the horrid noise of their closing jaws, their plunging amidst the broken ranks of fish, and rising with their prey some feet upright above the water, the floods of water and blood rushing out of their mouths and the clouds of vapour issuing from their wide nostrils, were truly frightful."

Audubon too, many years later, was impressed by the thrashing of alligator tails, which, he wrote, could be heard half a mile away, while the banks of the river in which the beasts massed were lined with ibises eating the injured fish that had managed to reach shore.

Fifty years ago no true Okefenokee man would have traveled anywhere in the swamp without carrying his gun and a pole shod with iron that he could use to beat back attacks on his boat by alligators seeking to seize his dogs. Today the alligators are not only fewer but also less likely to assault the boats of strange bipedal interlopers; dogs are no longer allowed in the swamp. "Just watch out you don't get near the nests," said Johnny Hickox, a quiet-spoken man whose family had been squeezed out of the swamp when it became a federal refuge in 1937, but who still never loses an opportunity to go back into it.

One day Johnny showed me how his father used to hunt alligators. He always worked on foot and when the water was low, as it was now, before the summer rains had begun. We walked along the shores of Cowhouse Island, in the north of the swamp, until we came to an alligator trail. It was nothing more than a muddy track running across the moss but we followed it, up to our knees in muck, until we came to a sinister-looking black pool, its edges frayed by the violence of its manufacture. "He's down in there, all right," Johnny said.

Sometimes, he told me, his father would "grunt" an alligator to the surface by imitating the animal's deep-throated growling noise, but more often he would insert a long pole into the water, holding one end between his teeth, lips parted, and grunt, the vibrations from his throat traveling down the pole and into the pool. Johnny demonstrated this technique with a stick I was carrying. Very soon—and, it seemed, obediently—our alligator surfaced, hard black eyes gleaming. "Now my daddy would shoot him," Johnny recalled. If grunting did not work, a large pole hook would be driven deep into the pool to snag the alligator. All alligator hunters were profoundly respectful of the toughness of the creature. "You couldn't be sure he was dead until you'd chopped into his backbone and cut through the spine," Johnny explained. An alligator not thoroughly dispatched in this way could come to life hours after lying apparently dead. The senior Hickox once shot an alligator three times and had it half skinned when it stirred, knocked him down, and began crawling back into the water.

To skin an alligator, he would turn it over, cut the belly skin down each side to the back legs, rip around the legs, and then slice down to the tail. The rest of the alligator was thrown away, to be eaten by other alligators or by the hordes of vultures that congregated at the swamp in the heyday of hunting. Sometimes, if the alligator was large and plump, Johnny's father might take a steak or two off the tail, but the weight of a good skin, about 20 pounds, plus the gun, the hatchet and a day's food, all made an exhausting load. Like any good hunter, he could stretch a green hide out another foot or so when he got it home, but with the 1930s price at between 60 and 80 cents a foot, he did not get rich from alligator hunting.

A pair of alligators feed and frolic near a riverbank in this drawing by the artist-naturalist William Bartram, made during his Southern explorations in the 1770s. Although Bartram never went into the Okefenokee itself, he was the first American writer to describe it with any sort of accuracy, basing his account on talks with local Indians.

When alligator hunters were not skinning the creatures for such small profit, they often amused themselves by baiting the alligators they had trapped. They would thrust a branch or stick into the alligator's jaws and then watch in delight as the animal turned itself over and over with savage speed. They used to say that "the gator's so mad, he jest can't control himself," and they thought that was pretty funny.

What they were watching was the alligator's trick of turning its long body into a powerful lever. When males fight for females, as they do throughout the swamp in late spring, they lock jaws and roll over and over in an attempt to exhaust each other. These fierce fights for the available females seem like terminal encounters to the untutored on-looker, yet few of them end in death when the contenders are approximately the same size. The object is to win the female, not to kill another male, and so the loser usually slides back into the water, blood-ied perhaps, but still hoping to attract another, unattached female. It is believed that the males find the females by following a scent trail—al-ligators emit a strong smell from cloacal glands.

As spring hurried along, breaking out bright green topknots on the cy-presses, a blush of flowers on the prairies, I pushed on through water-ways and lakes through a swamp transforming itself every day with new surges of life. I could not put down foot or canoe paddle without seeing all kinds of fish in the dark-brown, debris-filled water—dozens of them together in places—some infant, some adult, an illimitable un-derlayer that fed other kinds of fish as well as birds, raccoons, turtles and alligators.

The fish were spawning, and the water swarmed with tiny bodies. Was there room for more? The competition for space, food and refuge must be ferocious for vaulting new generations of pygmy sunfish, which are preyed on by the pickerel and gar and bass; for immeasurable swarms of minnows, which dart through every inch of surface water on every prairie; for pirate perch; for sunfish, large-mouthed bass, chub sucker and bowfin. The swamp is home for relatively few species of fish, less than 40, but it yields great quantities of them to fishermen each year. Georgians come buzzing into the swamp in their outboards hoping for large-mouthed bass (which they call trout), but more likely getting pickerel (which they call jackfish). I saw my first pygmy kil-lifish, one of the smallest fish on earth, an inch long fully grown, and wormlike. The Okefenokee is its ideal home, yet it was lost amid the millions of larger lives all around it. I could only guess what was hap-

The inflated pouch at the throat of this pinewoods tree frog—itself only about an inch and a half long—plays the role of the sound box in a guitar: filled with air, it adds resonance to the frog's trill. Only males have this sac, and they use it mostly to intensify their vocalizing during the mating season.

pening in the water under my canoe. Every time I boated down the watercourse fish leaped, sometimes several of them out of the water simultaneously. Beneath them, I guessed, was one of the realities of a cold-blooded world: a relentless thrusting of enemies.

The theme of death haunts the world of the cold-bloods. It gives a chill to the exuberance of spring, felt in the successive warming of days and sensed also in the growing host of frogs. During each trip I made into the swamp, frogs became a larger presence. They croaked at first, then massed their voices in a chorus that almost rivaled the alligators' cries; they whined, they clicked, they moaned. But I could visualize them being killed, gripped in the jaws of alligators, seized by cottonmouths, stalked by water birds—herons, ibises, egrets, anhingas. Cranes ate them and so did red-shouldered hawks. The frogs were eaten, in fact, by almost everything that could catch them. So were their amphibian cousins, the toads. Yet both frogs and toads came out of their primeval muck in an irresistible flow. Southern leopard frogs began to lay their plinths, columns of eggs stuck together, then came the long egg clusters of the southern toad and the bands of eggs of the eastern spadefoot. As March turned to April, a flood of eggs poured from squirrel tree frogs, cricket frogs, pinewoods tree frogs, little chorus frogs, carpenter frogs. The outflow of eggs went on ceaselessly and the early breeders were joined by new breeders—eastern gray tree frogs, narrow-mouthed toads, pig frogs. The breeding of many species would continue until early September.

During this tumultuous spring every expedition I made into the Okefenokee was a passage through an amusement park of frog sounds, absurd, exuberant, excited. One evening in April, soon after rain had swept the swamp, I walked along its western fringes through territory I had traveled a month earlier. Tiny ponds had sprung into view everywhere, each seeming to contain its complement of small shrill-voiced oak toads. There were hundreds of them visible. Some floated at the surface, arms held forward while they occasionally kicked themselves lethargically back and forth. From the fringes of the newly created ponds came the voices of colleagues who had not yet taken to water.

By nightfall of that day the impact of the frog and toad voices was stunning. It was such a mélange of sounds that no individual could be discerned, at least not by my untuned ears. Later, when I had had some coaching, I could recognize the components of the symphony. The cries that were almost like screams came from the oak toads. Behind these sounds was a kind of droning, like the background of a row of double basses playing a steady, single note in the orchestra; these were the southern toads singing. A steady clicking noise came from the cricket frog, an almost equally insect-like chirrup from the tiny chorus frog. The grunts and bleats, squeaks and metallic clangs of other species pursued me through the darkness.

The uproar of night voices had many daylight images, but they were incongruously small in the eyes after such a large assault on the ears. Southern cricket frogs, not much bigger than a penny, fled from under my feet in the boglands in a series of lightning-fast jumps that merged into one smooth arc of movement. A southern leopard frog sat on a lily leaf, the leaf trembling even though no water flowed around it and no wind was blowing. For a moment I thought a small alligator must be passing underneath, but when I looked more closely I saw a dark form, pointed upward, bumping the underside of the leaf. Perhaps the anonymous fish was eating algae from the leaf, but I preferred to believe that it was trying to nudge the frog off. The frog was not tempted.

On one expedition across the prairies I reached over the side of the canoe and caught a small alligator that held a pig frog in its sharp-toothed mouth and would not let go of it. The pig frog, similar to the southern bullfrog in size—nearly five inches long—had been betrayed by its love of prairies and cypress bays. Though it easily eludes the human hunter, it is no match for a hungry alligator. I tossed the alligator back into the water, its teeth still clamped on its prey. Its narrow head disappeared beneath the surface while the frog's webbed hind feet twitched spasmodically. I caught a glimpse of the frog's spotted belly—a flash of black, brown, yellow—and it was gone. Nearby, another pig frog floated on the surface of the water, grunting. Here among the amphibians of the Okefenokee, existence is shorn of feelings of pain, stripped to the stark essentials of life and death.

When showers fled across the swamp the toads massed for new prodigies of effort. In the cloying heat after the showers, moisture dripped from every bush and tree and stem of grass and formed temporary ponds in which oak toads, wearing coats of many colors, predominated. As I walked along, their piercing peeps gradually blurred into a continuous scream that carried an almost emotional impact. I could imagine desperation, urgency, hysteria in the oak toad's voice. Behind the voices flowed an avalanche of eggs. At night the breeding toads clearly revealed themselves, oblivious to my presence. They floated everywhere in shallow water, expelling eggs. Sometimes the eggs trailed from their

Frogs and toads, 21 kinds in all, are the most numerous amphibians in the swamp and the noisiest. The air is full of their soprano trills, raucous tenor barks and deep bass grunts. The sounds are at their height at breeding time, but since breeding goes on all year in the case of some species, the decibel count seldom drops much.

Though the creatures vary widely in their markings, it is frequently impossible, even for most experts, to distinguish between certain frogs because some species are similar in color and even change color. It is a lot easier to tell a frog from a toad: as a rule, if it hops rather than leaps, and if the skin is dry and warty, it's a toad.

WEB-FOOTED PIG FROG

THUMB-SIZED SQUIRREL TREE FROG

WART-COVERED OAK TOAD

BARKING TREE FROG

bodies and were caught in the stems of half-submerged grasses. Slimy streams of eggs lay limp along the strands of the temporary ponds.

This affirmation of life, displayed on such a generous scale, was flawed. Perhaps there was urgency in those voices, for the toads live dangerously. They cannot know how long their pools of breeding water will last. Each summer is different. Some are wet throughout. In other years, the pools dry out as early as June. The toads must go through their mating act while the water remains deep enough to foster their tadpoles to the point where they can reach dry land on their own. As it happened, this year the toads were to be unlucky. A few weeks later I saw the pools drying prematurely and an entire new generation of toads was wiped out.

Old swampers believed that the voice of the oak toad was actually that of a black snake calling out. Although their faulty natural history was later corrected by visiting experts, I liked their fanciful version. Those high-pitched voices, not toadlike at all, were more satisfying to imagine as coming from throngs of singing snakes. And the peeping of the toads did indeed seem to coincide with the appearance of many snakes. In the early spring I never saw a snake in the swamp. By April they were as busy in their way as the frogs, and thus more visible—as well as vulnerable. One day I watched an osprey carrying a small snake into a nearby tree and a tiny alligator struggling with another small snake among some lilies. I canoed among shaded cypresses toward a brilliant patch of sunlight. A cottonmouth basked there, draped over an eye-level branch. It looked directly at me. Its eyes had no lids and the pupils, thin slits of deep green that could expand at night for hunting, were now contracted to protect the eyes' sensitive interiors. I skirted the snake slowly; one of the hazards of travel in the old days was the danger of basking snakes falling into passing boats. But today there is very little danger of acquiring an unwanted serpent passenger if one follows the marked boat trails. Snakes are secretive by nature and have learned to avoid the tourist trails.

Like all the other cold-bloods, the snakes become active mainly at night and so I could only glimpse their domain. At dusk one day I watched a raccoon working its way steadily along the shores of Honey Island, feeling for crayfish in the muck, its delicate fingers squeezing each handful of mud for food. Suddenly, it jerked backward and the body of a snake went spinning away. This was egg-laying time for some snakes: king snakes, racers, pine snakes and indigos. Walking at night, I constantly had to watch underfoot for snakes traveling in search of sandy egg-burial places, and for the cottonmouths, rattlers and water snakes, which bear their young alive.

I had no wish to try to distinguish between a venomous cottonmouth and a harmless water snake in the dark—a difficult enough identification even in bright sunlight, since cottonmouths look like many nonpoisonous water snakes except for the deep pits they have between eyes and nostrils. Also, many water snakes are about as long as cottonmouths, around three feet, with dark topsides and lighter bellies. The cottonmouth, however, invariably reveals itself by its more aggressive response. The timid water snake flees, but the cottonmouth holds fast, rears its head and opens its mouth to reveal the pure white inside that has given the snake its name. Like many snakes when aroused, it will vibrate its tail, and if it has been surprised among dry twigs the sound effect can be daunting, a low and sinister chatter.

Among the water snakes, the brown is the one most frequently mistaken for a cottonmouth. Its head is broader than its neck, and when viewed from certain perspectives appears to be diamond-shaped—an attribute that is widely but wrongly supposed to identify venomous snakes only. Browns climb trees and like to bask on branches sometimes 20 feet above the ground. But most of all the brown is a skilled swimmer and takes its food from the water or the surrounding land.

Oddly, because the Okefenokee is a snake paradise, very few snakes show themselves, and very few insights can be gained into their lives from a few months, or even years, of watching. But the little that can be observed of their habits suggests a beautifully organized world. One of the least visible snakes is the nonpoisonous eastern king snake, a sleek dark serpent with a pattern of pale links on its scales. Though occasionally it will bask or travel in the open, it is essentially nocturnal and tends to conceal itself. Its average length is under four feet, though it has been known to grow to nearly seven feet—a fact that increases its threat as a powerful constrictor. The king snake is immune to the venom of the poisonous species and kills them as efficiently as it dispatches the harmless varieties—wrapping itself around its prey and squeezing it to death.

Much more often visible during the day is the slender nonvenomous southern black racer, which measures an average of about four feet and can be identified by the touches of white at its throat. This subspecies is one of the fastest-moving snakes in the swamp, and when it is aroused the sound of its tail vibrations could almost be that of a rattler. The racer has its own lethal way of dealing with its victims —usually rodents, small lizards and other snakes: it throws a loop over its prey and pins it down, much like a wrestler.

Each Okefenokee snake fits neatly into a very specific niche by reason of either habit or appearance. The Florida pine snake is the color of the sand that is its preferred habitat. Its head, with a pointed snout, seems too small for the large constricting body, which averages about five feet. Though it is nonpoisonous, this snake puts on quite a show at the approach of an enemy: its hiss is highly audible and it strikes without hesitation. Pocket gophers and other small burrowing creatures are frequently its victims because of its ability to go in after them.

One of my favorite snakes in the swamp—it earns the watcher's admiration—is the eastern coachwhip, a day-loving snake that is often very visible and sometimes spectacular in its movements. The coachwhip, which gets its name from the appearance of its long tail, can put on extraordinary speed in order to escape danger from a predator such as a swift-plunging hawk. But when there is no escape, it will go on the attack, sinking its fangs in, then wrenching them out, severely lacerating its enemy.

Almost every confrontation with a snake presented a surprise. Once, in the depths of thick shrubbery on an island, I nearly stepped on an indigo that, because of its great size—nearly six feet long—sent me jumping back hurriedly while it hissed, shook its tail and flattened its neck. Yet this beautiful snake, a glossy blue-black all over, is almost totally harmless to man. I could have picked it up and risked small chance of a bite. For all that, this is a snake that eats not only mice, rats, birds and frogs, but also cottonmouths and rattlers. Like the black racer, it pins its victims down with loops of its body.

The three rattlers of the Okefenokee, in ascending order of size, are the pygmy, which is less than two feet long, the canebrake, which can grow to five feet, and the eastern diamondback, which averages about six feet, and is one of the deadliest snakes anywhere. Meeting it is unforgettable because of the intensity of its response. Its rattle cannot be confused with that of any other snake in the Okefenokee; in a mature diamondback the vibration of its tail will cause the horny segments of the tail to strike against one another with a sound that is itself chilling. Added to this is the special menace of the broad wavering head and the strong, tightly wound coils, all suggesting that the serpent is about to make a lightning-fast leap forward.

An eastern coachwhip twines a maple branch, ready to inflict a vicious though nonvenomous bite if cornered. Like a rattler, it vibrates its tail when threatened, but silently. And contrary to myth, the coachwhip does not use its tail as a lash.

Turtles, too, fit into the life of the swamp with intricate, small details of adaptation. One day, walking along the sandy edge of an island, I saw what looked like a flattened brown dome gliding along the ground ahead of me toward the water. It was a turtle, but moving at a rate of speed quite unturtle-like. This Florida softshell, the biggest of all the North American softshells, was almost a foot long, and its bumpy carapace sliced into the water like a miniature spaceship submerging. Softshell is a deceptive name for these irritable creatures, which, when caught or prevented from reaching the sanctuary of water, can be damaging adversaries with their sharp claws and powerful mandibles. Nobody seems quite sure why their carapaces should bend freely at the sides and back, like well-tanned leather, though this flexibility seems yet another subtle survival device that may permit the turtle to slip away from a predator. Occasionally in shallow water I would see the eyes and snout of a softshell protruding, the rest of the body concealed beneath the surface. When the creature needed air, it would stretch up its long neck until its nostrils reached the surface.

On another day a swirl of water showed ahead of my canoe. At first I thought it was an alligator moving, but when I looked into the brown water a huge bulk passed quickly, misshapen like a chunk of folded lava. It was an alligator snapper that weighed about 150 pounds. This species is the swamp's largest turtle; it is, in fact, one of the largest fresh-water species in the world. Its ugly pointed head, vicious hooked beak and size make it unique among turtles. Its shell—rough in youth but smoother and deeply ridged in adulthood—is a dark brown and its tail, like that of all snapping turtles, is very long, sometimes even longer than its body, and useful for swimming. To entrap its fish food, the alligator snapper employs a curious cylindrical growth at the bottom of its mouth. Ordinarily whitish, this growth turns pink when it is moved; the turtle will lie in the water with its mouth open and wiggle the little appendage, attracting fish that mistake it for a worm.

Later I saw a tiny loggerhead musk turtle slipping through the water. It was no more than four inches long, its light head daubed with darker spots. These turtles are also called stink-jims—for good reason. When alarmed, they emit an evil-smelling substance from two body openings.

The turtles, like the rest of the cold-bloods, are an expression of unchanged survival over millions of years. In other seasons they appear static and dull, endlessly sunning themselves on logs. But in the springtime, they are galvanized into their one assertive act of the year, when they have to leave the water to lay their eggs.

The survival of the frogs I could understand because they simply out-breed their many enemies. But the turtles must lay their eggs just at the time young bears, born in January or February, are beginning to learn to hunt independently. Turtle eggs help them to get started. Almost any-place where the swamp had compacted into a semblance of dry ground, particularly along the banks of the Suwannee Canal, turtles were at work trying to dig secure places for their eggs. At night the shores of the canal were patrolled by raccoons and bears that just as assiduously dug out the eggs. It was a perfect study in futility, made all the more im-pressive by the response of the turtles. They laid more eggs.

Almost exactly the same thing was happening on the swamp islands and along their edges. Turtles heaved themselves out of the water at night to find dry-land repositories for their eggs. Raccoons marked the passage of the turtles inland; and snakes, too, watched them, or so I pre-sumed, because it was uncanny how quickly the buried eggs were uncovered. Sometimes, even as the turtles were digging holes for egg-laying, a snake waited nearby, curled up and patient, while a raccoon dozed in a tree close by. Once the eggs were laid and covered and the turtle had gone back to the water, the feast began. Among the feasters, the nonvenomous king snakes often ate entire clutches of up to 20 eggs. They uncovered the eggs with their heads and mouths, then gaped their flexible jaws to eat.

With the competition for eggs so severe, the turtles had resorted to sub-terfuge. The Florida cooters laid their eggs in alligator nests that were still being heaped up, six feet in diameter and two or three feet out of the water. The gopher tortoise, a brown-shelled creature less than a foot long whose front legs can fold to protect the head and neck against attack, dug a sloping burrow for its eggs in the dry pine barrens along the eastern fringe of the swamp. At the end of the burrow, which can be 20 or 30 feet deep, she dug a space large enough to turn around in. There she was joined from time to time by gopher frogs, burrowing owls, raccoons, diamondback rattlers, southern toads, gopher-hole crickets, various spiders and flies. A tick would also enter the burrow, rousing itself from time to time to suck the tortoise's blood. Other tem-porary guests might include the pine snake, the six-lined race-runner lizard, the cottontail rabbit, the coachwhip snake, the indigo snake, and perhaps even an occasional skunk, opossum or gray fox.

Here, in this bitter straining for egg sanctuary, was contained one rea-son that the earth eventually became the domain of warm-blooded creatures. Those vulnerable eggs invited the evolution of quicker-witted, faster-moving egg hunters. In midsummer in the Okefenokee, alligator eggs would be gobbled up at almost the same rate as those of the turtles. By then the alligators would have hundreds of nests dotted throughout the swamp, some built in dense shrubbery in prairie hammocks, others in open water, consisting of nothing more than mounds of heaped-up vegetation. Some alligators would go into the middle of the islands and dig out nests in low-lying boggy patches. It would not matter much where the alligators put the nests—the bears would find them. If the bears did not, the raccoons would. In some places more than half of every 100 nests might be pillaged even though the female alligator rarely moves far from her nest and can be vicious in its defense.

The outpouring of eggs would continue as the young began hatching around the end of August. Quite suddenly the reptile would become a different creature. Until I saw them, I did not believe anything could be quite so pretty or so touching as the appearance of young alligators in the bright sun. At the grunt cry of the first-born the female alligator would tear the nest to pieces. The youngsters that emerged looked like miniature dragons, beautifully marked, their skin sleek as silk, their jaws like small spring-actuated toys. I got a disarming view of alligator life when I saw a mother herding her babies together with the solicitude of a warm-blooded animal. She basked, her back covered with sunning youngsters; they would stay with her for several months before taking off into the swamp waters by themselves.

Turtles, too, were hatching. They came out of canal-side nests and slipped into the water. They emerged from nests in hammocks, under the deep shade of magnolia and live oak, and headed for the water. They burst out of the sand of Billy's Island, and Honey Island, and Cowhouse Island, and turned unerringly toward the water at night, often in blinding rain. The people of the swamp used to amuse themselves by turning the hatchlings around, blocking their paths with branches. But nothing short of death deterred them. The road to the water was far older than the swamp itself.

During all of the springtime of the cold-bloods I had slowly become accustomed to the noise of the alligators. I had learned that when the bellowing swelled to a crescendo it was mating time and the bulls were defending their own turf. Once, as I stood in Territory Prairie, a fighter plane passed over the swamp, breaking the sound barrier, and its boom brought a responding roar from the Okefenokee as dozens of alligators challenged this man-made noise. It was a chilling moment, that world of dinosaurs roaring back at the world of computers. Old swampers had told me that if I listened carefully I could hear the different types of alligator call. I did not immediately develop such refined ears but in time I began to realize that each alligator voice was a shade different from any other, possibly because of differences in size. This led to the skin-prickling conclusion that perhaps individual alligators could recognize each other, sight unseen, and that there might be a whole world of communication out there, beyond my powers of comprehension.

In a dark pool hidden in a cypress bay a solitary male alligator surfaced at twilight, his knobbled back as ancient-looking as the length of his ancestral past. This time I was so close to the reptile that when he bellowed it was like being struck a blow. He roared again and again. Each time a savage reply echoed from the southern end of the prairie. Sitting there as night fell, I wondered who was listening to him, who was replying. Was he giving an order for a female to come to a designated meeting place? But it was late June now and almost all the breeding was done. Was he roaring a warning that he possessed this territory, and was some other alligator challenging his authority? Or was he bellowing just for the sake of making a noise, roaring at the pleasure of being alive? If so, why the faithful response?

The roaring continued off and on through the night, then stopped as the sky lightened at four o'clock. Perhaps the alligator had tired from his exertions, or perhaps he was gathering strength for another round. In the sudden silence, no answering sound came now from the other end of the prairies. And in the predawn light, the pool whence he had called was empty, smooth and black.

A Refuge for Reptiles

More than any other wild region of North America, the Okefenokee Swamp is a stunning reminder of the great age of reptiles, when scaly creatures ranging from lizards to dinosaurs dominated the earth. Lizards still flourish in the swamp, along with myriad snakes and turtles —but the dinosaur has yielded its preeminent place to the alligator.

As they were in more ancient times, the lizards are generally the smallest, gentlest and least predatory of the Okefenokee's reptiles, living chiefly on the millions of insects they consume every year. The snakes, however, justify every warning urged on the swamp visitor. Some of the most venomous varieties known in the United States live here: coral snakes, cottonmouths and rattlesnakes lurk beneath fallen logs, in the underbrush and around old tree stumps, ready to lunge at the approach of man or beast. Each of the snake species follows its own special diet, but collectively they devour, among other things, insects, worms, fish, crayfish, frogs, toads, lizards, rodents, raccoons, birds and other snakes. Extremely prolific—as many as 75 offspring are produced a year—the snakes could easily take over the swamp in a few years if

they were not, in turn, the prey of alligators and other creatures.

Turtles have remained relatively unchanged since dinosaur times, about 200 million years ago. After eons of survival, the larger species almost met their doom when man discovered how edible the meat was under that shell—although some varieties are more succulent than others. In the guarded seclusion of such wildlife refuges as the Okefenokee, however, they thrive and proliferate. The swamp shelters 15 kinds of turtles in a self-contained environment where they feed on fresh-water shrimp, lizards, snakes, water plants and other victuals, and need fear only such natural foes as the bear and the alligator.

Alligators, the naturalists believe, will eat almost anything, including every other denizen of the swamp and their own young. They, like the turtles, date back to the Triassic Period when the reptiles ruled. In the Okefenokee today the alligators reign supreme, their only enemies a large bear or an occasional human poacher. But even the poacher risks danger; if he drops his guard the alligator may seize his arm and, with a rapid spinning motion, wrench it from his shoulder.

In peaceful proximity, an alligator and a Florida cooter share a corner of the swamp. Ordinarily this species of turtle would provide a quick mouthful for its hefty neighbor, but when the weather is cold in the Okefenokee the digestive system of the alligator is dormant, thus depriving the beast of its appetite.

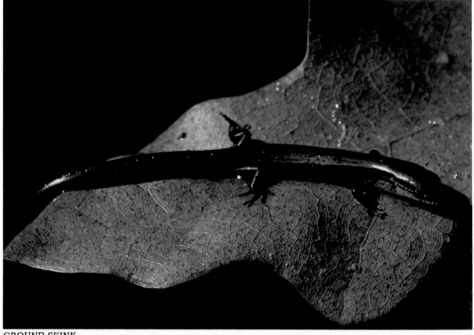

GROUND SKINK

EASTERN SLENDER GLASS LIZARD

A Profusion of Darting Lizards

Anyone who has a squeamish reaction to lizards would have a hard time of it in the Okefenokee. The swamp is home to at least 11 different lizard species, from three inches to more than three feet long. They are there in countless numbers, exploring the vegetation for opportunities to reduce the insect population and trying to avoid a similar fate for themselves.

Prized items in the diet of all the other reptiles living in the swamp, the lizards have developed ways and means to cope with would-be predators. One species, the ground skink *(top left)* has an effective escape mechanism if caught by its tail; it simply pulls away, leaving the tail behind. The glass lizard *(bottom left)*, often mistaken for a snake because it is legless, nevertheless is able to slither away from danger at full speed. Swiftest and perhaps most elusive of Okefenokee lizards is the six-lined race runner, which is capable of such a fast getaway that it is known locally as the race nag.

But the most artful dodger of the lizard clan is the green anole, often called the American chameleon *(right)*. A skilled climber of small deciduous trees, it can dart around branches to befuddle a pursuer. And in or out of trees it employs a better-known weapon of defense. Because special pigment cells in its skin react to heat, light and fright, it can change color—thus often successfully camouflaging its presence.

A SIX-INCH GREEN ANOLE, ALIAS THE AMERICAN CHAMELEON

COMMON SNAPPING TURTLE

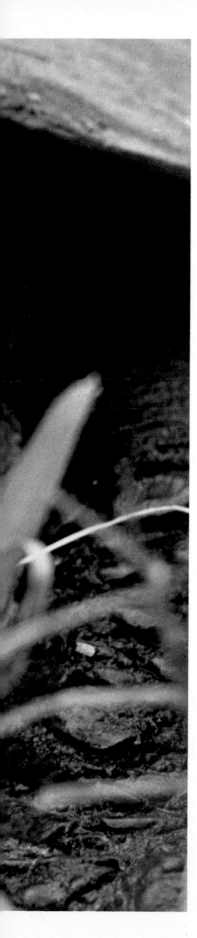

Turtles of Different Temper

Temperamentally speaking, Okefenokee turtles divide into the mean and the mild, with the mean species in a fearsome minority of three. The common snapping turtle *(left)* announces its ugly disposition with its menacing grimace and its readiness to attack anything in sight. The scarcer alligator snapper—so called for the gator-like ridges on its back —is less aggressive, but when provoked it will utilize jaws strong enough to break a small boy's arm. Largest of the fresh-water turtles, it can weigh 150 pounds or more.

The third fierce species in the swamp, the Florida soft-shelled turtle *(right, center)*, is also the fastest swimmer. It lives in the deepest parts of streams and lakes, feeding on frogs, fish and waterfowl that it nabs by means of a sharp beak and a long flexible neck, and it comes ashore only to bask or lay eggs. Strangely, softshells seem to be found wherever there are alligators. Their speed and ability to defend themselves with powerful mandibles may explain such odd fellowship.

Among the harmless species of turtle in the swamp are the box turtles and the cooters. Box turtles, their black or brown shells vividly spotted yellow, orange or olive, prefer life on land but will soak for hours in mud or water. Cooters love to bask but are extremely wary and thus hard to catch. When caught, however, they show their innate gentleness and are entirely amiable.

FLORIDA BOX TURTLE

FLORIDA SOFTSHELL LAYING EGGS

BABY FLORIDA COOTERS BASKING

Snakes: The Patient Predators

No fewer than 38 kinds of snakes prowl the Okefenokee, ranging in size from the seven-inch rough earth snake to the eight-foot eastern indigo. Three of the four poisonous serpent groups of North America are represented in the swamp: the cottonmouth (the most numerous); the rattlesnake, including the dusky pigmy, the canebrake *(bottom right)* and the eastern diamondback; and the gaily banded coral snake *(top right)*, cousin of the cobra. Only the copperhead is absent.

Whether venomous or not, all the snakes of the swamp are predators, equipped with elastic lower jaws that can gape wide enough to ingest prey far larger than the diameter of their bodies. Nor do they draw the line at consuming their own kind. A pair of king snakes can start eating from opposite ends of the same piece of food; when their heads meet, one will go on to devour the other. Fortunately for the creatures that are their favored eating, most snakes have slow metabolisms that enable them to go for extended stretches of time without food.

At least three times a year, and oftener in the case of some species, Okefenokee snakes shed their skins to accommodate growth—and they do a thorough job of it, as demonstrated by the yellow rat snake shown opposite. The snake divests itself of its entire epidermis in one piece, including even the transparent scales covering its eyes.

EASTERN CORAL SNAKE

A CANEBRAKE RATTLESNAKE ABOUT TO STRIKE

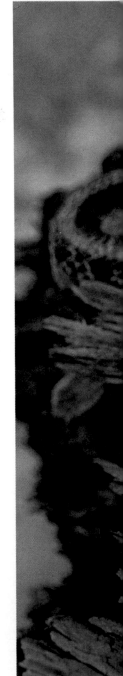

A YELLOW RAT SNAKE SHEDDING ITS SKIN

Masters of All They Survey

According to the accounts of Okefenokee pioneers, the virgin swamp was so chock-full of alligators that a daring hunter could run across a stream or pond on their backs. Subsequently the great beasts fell on hard times when men relentlessly slaughtered them for their skins; in 1906, by one estimate, large skins fetched $1.50 apiece, a rate that encouraged a lot of killing.

In recent decades, however, the Okefenokee alligator population has remained relatively stable at about 10,000, thanks in part to the swamp's establishment as a safeguarded refuge and in part to the Federal Endangered Species Act.

The nesting habits of the alligators also tend to increase their numbers. Each year the female lays from 11 to 60 eggs in a carefully assembled mound of decaying vegetation. She does not sit on the nest, since the heat generated by the decay suffices to hatch the eggs, but unlike most female reptiles she keeps a close eye on matters. When the young are about to pop out of their shells, she clears away the nest cover and fusses over her brood. Then the maternal care becomes more casual; after two or three months the hatchlings are on their own, prey to snakes and other alligators. However, if they survive these perils and grow to maturity they join an omnivorous, highly mobile ruling class that holds undisputed sway over the reptile world of the Okefenokee.

AN ADULT MALE ALLIGATOR BEHIND A BED OF POND LILIES

3/ Man's Fleeting Traces

It was not their voices that reached over the swamp, only echoes. . . . But, as they loosed the signal call, it struck upon the water drum of Okefenokee, and the vast resounding surface rolled it on. CECILE HULSE MATSCHAT/ SUWANNEE RIVER

It is May 1912, and two swampers stand in a pond near Billy's Island. The shallow water ripples at their shins and the cypresses are distorted in ragged reflections behind them. One man is gripping a long pole with both hands, his mouth over one end of the pole as he grunts into it, the other end of the pole is a dozen feet away in the water. He is trying to summon up an alligator by voice vibrations. The man next to him tensely holds a revolver. In a moment another alligator dies.

The people of the Okefenokee cannot be separated from its natural history because they are an integral part of it. Some outsiders looking at the swampers during the 19th Century thought that they were simply ignorant and backward. Others took a darker view. In their opinion, the swampers had turned their backs on civilization and had chosen to live in an awful, primitive, lawless place where men could not be trusted and women wore paint like Indians. In fact, the tight enclave formed by the swampers was neither quite civilized nor quite primitive. These people were Anglo-Saxons with a dash of Huguenot, primitive Baptist Church folk, more familiarly known as Hard Shells. And hard they were. It took me a while to see enough of their islands and travel far enough in their swamp to be able to measure that quality of toughness and endurance.

But to re-create them is not so easy. Some descendants of the true swamp dwellers—men who lived within the swamp itself—still live around its fringes. They are straightforward, pragmatic people who share a common pride in the fact that their forebears were masters of a world that accepted only the hardiest and most determined of men.

The pictures preserved of the swampers give the same feeling of unreality as passing through the swamp itself. They glide along in their clumsy puntlike boats, poling a harvest of turpentine gathered from the pinewoods along their "roadways" winding through the swamp. They can be seen at dawn lined up with their old rifles and beat-up shotguns, mongrel dogs yapping around them as they plan the day's hunting strategy. They are shown as youngsters, back from fishing with 30 large warmouths on a string.

In the early decades of the 20th Century they impressed Francis Harper, a Cornell University scientist, as a "sturdy, self-sufficient" people who built their dwellings from the logs of longleaf pine, lit their way around their houses with blazing pine knots, grew corn, potatoes, peanuts and sugar cane and lived on the meat of their cattle, their razorback hogs, their hunting of deer, possums, raccoons, squirrels, quail, wild turkeys and turtles, and their catches of all kinds of fish. Everything went into the pot. A bear unwise enough to get caught in the act of attacking the hogs would almost certainly be eaten by the hogs' owner. There was plenty of honey in hollow cypress logs or in bee gums. When the swampers needed money for guns or traps, they sold the skins of alligators, bobcats and otters.

They occupied their kingdom with the same kind of superstitious reverence that had touched earlier visitors to the Okefenokee. But instead of the "daughters of the sun" William Bartram had reported to be living there, the swampers enlivened evenings at home with tales of demons lurking on every island in the dead of night. They spoke, tongue in cheek, of the black snake that could sing the sweetest lullaby human ears had ever heard; when a man lured by this seductive song followed the black snake, he was bitten and killed by the "old diamondback" that lurked near the siren-singer. The Indians, the swampers told visitors with straight faces, were so "extree" fond of honey they wed bumblebees to lightning bugs (fireflies) so that the hybrid insects would work in the dark; that way, there was more honey for everybody.

Their isolation and their total mastery of swamp resources made them truly people of the wilderness, aware of all its nuances. Bird songs were listened to intently. The hooting of the barred owl signaled that it was feeding time for animals. The chattering of woodpeckers in the open pinewoods indicated that the fish were biting.

An early-20th Century logger hauls a gator from the depths as a coworker watches. The sale of gator skin augmented their meager pay.

The swampers had to be expert navigators. It was just as easy to get lost in the swamp then as it is today. The oldtimers found their way by noting tiny differences in the growth of bark on trees, a technique so difficult it required years of study. Another method was to spot the nests of the swamp's many ospreys. The swampers had learned that each pair of birds staked out their own prairie. Because each nest was about four miles from the next one, a swamper who could recognize the shapes of individual nests knew immediately where he was.

In the early summer an old swamper demonstrated the music of his people for me, a kind of yodeling that they called hollerin', and that later became known as the grand opera of the Okefenokee. The sounds of his voice slapped against the cypresses in a series of hollow echoes. The shrill cries were pushed from the front of the throat and were so piercing they carried for miles. The swamp people had favorite hollerin' times—at daybreak and sunset, when a hunter returned home safe or simply to express exuberance.

Hollerin' was also a distinctive signature. It allowed a local man to travel at night and not be shot if he set foot on another man's island. The enduring legend of the swamp is that it was the haunt of the lawless, a place of murders where an outsider's life was valueless the moment he intruded. Murder in the swamp was almost impossible to prove, however, because the victim invariably was fed to the alligators. His disappearance was explained as emigration to other parts. The swampers themselves, although defensive about legends of lawlessness in their domain, admitted some "justifiable killing." If a man were caught spying on moonshiners, for instance, he could hardly expect to avoid a bullet in the brain.

The swamp folk created their own family dynasties, each with its special quality, usually based on the personality of its founder. Josiah Mizell, who founded one of these families, had an insatiable curiosity about the swamp. During the early 1870s he devised a new way to explore its unknown parts. Until that time, men got about by wading through the shallows, or jumping from one patch of bog to another, or pushing through water that reached up to their armpits. Josiah designed a special boat, the forerunner of all swamp boats. It was made of cypress, and was 12 feet long and three feet wide—a utility boat that could take two men and their dogs, guns, blankets, sweet potatoes and bacon, and was thus both transportation and a floating campsite. In it Mizell could stay out in the swamp for days or weeks at a time.

Here was the perfect vehicle for penetrating the wilderness, riding so lightly on the water that it could be poled over the top of floating weeds. Josiah carried an eight-foot-long pole, to the end of which was fastened his Civil War bayonet. His son Hamp, writing of those days years later, explained that the bayonet was used to fight off the alligators that would, at times, fight the boat and try to drag off the dogs.

Operating from the eastern fringes of the swamp, Josiah navigated the same narrow reaches of water I later traveled, penetrating ever deeper into the Okefenokee. In time he reached the place now known as Chase Prairie, which is about six miles long and three miles wide. He saw deer and black bear along its shores, and was astounded by the numbers of ducks and "whooping cranes"—actually sandhill cranes. The whole prairie appeared to be a vast hunting preserve. The animals had been so long insulated from men that they were quite tame.

Josiah and his friends hunted Chase Prairie for years, then explored south through boglands and eventually found Bugaboo Island, one of the most inaccessible of all the swamp's islands. The men had hardly made camp when an uproar broke out. Their dogs had cornered a cougar. In the fight the dogs were thrashed and routed. The hunters slept uneasily. About two hours later another fight started and this time two of the dogs were nearly killed. The men were now so thoroughly frightened that they established military-style watches, "for they did not know how many of these deadly dangerous panthers were on this newly discovered island," Hamp Mizell later wrote.

When Josiah and his party explored the next morning they found several fresh deer kills, carefully covered with dead grass as protection against the omnipresent vultures. This discovery made them even more nervous; they knew such camouflage was the work of cougars, which then kept watch on their concealed kills and might attack any man, or any other animal, daring to interfere with them. After a conference, the men decided to keep the location of Bugaboo a secret. Before they left they set fire to it to burn off dry undergrowth and dead leaves and thus make their next hunting visit easier.

They later set up a permanent camp, but the secret of Bugaboo Island was revealed when one man took some other friends there. These visitors, furious that they had been kept from such great hunting for so many years, took it out on the camp. They burned down the buildings and put bullet holes through the pots. Later, elsewhere in the swamp, they smashed all the boats they could find belonging to Mizell and his men. There is no record of Josiah's reaction but it must have been severe indeed, because the interlopers never again set foot on Bugaboo Island.

It is a mistake to expect that men living closer to the earth will somehow be more noble, more ethical, more honorable than city dwellers. But the swamp people whose footsteps I was following had their fine qualities: determination, strength of character, a sense of identity, simple values and beliefs, and physical toughness. It was a necessary toughness. Years ago the father of Johnny Hickox—the man who showed me how to hunt alligators—was hunting a raccoon that had disappeared around the other side of a tree. He put a loaded shotgun between his legs and reached up to clap his hands to scare the raccoon. The gun went off and blew off his right hand just above the wrist. Hickox had to walk three miles to his home, then be taken four miles to a place where the doctor could reach him.

Toughness was not merely essential to survival; it was a deliberate way of life. One swamper, John Craven, roamed the Okefenokee without shelter, blanket or ground cover, ignoring icy winter winds and heavy rains. He got sick only once and then, he claimed, because he had to be a witness at a court trial in the village of Waycross. He complained bitterly about the terrible air inside the hotel room and almost immediately got a severe cold that he blamed on the "unhealthy" conditions outside the swamp.

The names of some islands of the swamp suggest its human history. Roasting Ear Island, along the southeast fringes of the swamp, was discovered with mature corn growing on it in the 19th Century. The corn was probably a relic of the presence of Civil War deserters who hid out on Roasting Ear and nearby Soldiers Camp Island. A slave was once stolen from his owner and kept prisoner on what became known as John's Negro Island. Chesser Island, south of the Suwannee Canal entrance, and the second-largest island in the swamp, was named after W. T. Chesser, a Georgia farmer who settled it in 1858. He cleared away part of its dense growth of yellow pines and began a farming dynasty of hunters, trappers and guides who knew the Okefenokee, one account recalls, "as well as a street urchin knows the streets of a large city." Chesser's corn sprouted from a field tilled on an ancient Indian mound. The light, sandy quality of its soil produced sugar cane whose syrup was famous for its flavor, clarity and golden color.

Cowhouse Island, which hugs the northernmost fringe of the swamp and is headquarters for the privately owned Okefenokee Swamp Park, is the most accessible island in the swamp, along with Chesser, and the largest, nine miles long and two miles wide. It is hardly an island at all, but an extension of the sandy land of Ware County, separated from it by some swampy ground. Cowhouse was so named because local farmers kept cattle there; it provided excellent winter grazing, its trees protecting the cattle from prevailing northwest winds. Gradually the island was populated and finally dominated by a prosperous farming family, the Crews, whose members became so numerous that the county built a school on Cowhouse chiefly for their children.

Other Okefenokee islands, too, felt the imprint of man, but none more dramatically than the one known as Billy's Island. In the early 19th Century a band of Seminole used it as a base in a last-ditch fight against white domination; by the end of the century, it had become the site of a boomtown, the center of an enterprise aimed at stripping the swamp of its treasure of lumber. That effort had long since ended, and wilderness reigned again. No exploration of the Okefenokee, I knew, could be counted complete without a journey to Billy's Island.

The name itself pays homage to a man who, as legend has it, showed a perfect understanding of the swamp: Billy Bowlegs, a Seminole who made camp on the island during the second half of the 18th Century. Billy's origins are disputed. Some historians believe that he was the son of a white man and an Indian woman; some others say that his father was a Secoffee, who had founded the Seminole tribe by leading a breakaway group from the main body of Creek Indians. The Seminole thus became double renegades, seeking independence from the Creek tribe and the white man, and a group of them, led by Billy Bowlegs, took their stand in the Okefenokee islands.

Billy was determined never to be caught by the government troops that were pursuing him, and he never was caught. He was a native guerrilla who understood that the white men would destroy his world if they could. His darting forays out of the swamp were ruthless. Women, children, men and animals were slaughtered indiscriminately in raids that left from Billy's Island. Finally, in 1838, the Indian massacres became unbearable to the white settlers rimming the swamp, and General Charles Floyd of the United States Army invaded the Okefenokee. Floyd and his men marched the length of Billy's Island but found no one. Billy and his followers had escaped to the Everglades.

Less than two decades later, before the Civil War, Billy's Island had its first white settler. Daniel Lee built a cabin there, cleared enough land to grow corn, potatoes and sugar cane, and made an added living by fishing, hunting and trapping. He also sired 16 children, 14 of whom

The story of Billy Bowlegs, shown here in full Seminole regalia, is shrouded in myth. According to local lore he was squat, powerfully built and bowlegged—hence his name. But most probably "Bowlegs" was a family appellation or a white man's nickname. Some historians believe he was a half-breed, the son of a white man who committed a crime and escaped into the swamp.

survived to adulthood. The Lee family line remained on the island until the 1930s, long enough to see the lumber entrepreneurs come and go, and to see their stronghold begin to revert to its natural state.

Billy's Island lies almost dead center in the swamp. It is accessible along an odd tongue of sand called The Pocket, which projects from the west into the swamp and is flanked by navigable water. These natural factors have made the island a center around which much of the rest of the swamp rotates like planets around their sun, and I wanted very much to see it.

Planning the trip with two veterans of Okefenokee exploration, I realized that an easy way to reach Billy's Island was to canoe directly south from Cowhouse, a journey that would take us through the center of the swamp, down a long reach of water that joins a series of lakes and is actually one of the tributary beginnings of the Suwannee River. But there was a more roundabout route, and I chose it because I wanted to see the man-made canal I had followed from the air. We decided to canoe only part of the way south from Cowhouse, then cut east to Floyd's Island. From there we could visit Chase Prairie, where Josiah Mizell and his friends had hunted, and from it reach the Suwannee Canal. Once on the canal, we could travel almost due west and, when we reached its limits, force our way through the overgrown waterways to reach Billy's Island.

So the three of us set out in a canoe. Jimmy Walker is a well-known local folksinger and chief executive of the Okefenokee Swamp Park. He is an urbane Georgian whose great-grandfather was a swamp dweller, the fierce and redoubtable Obediah Barber, known as King of the Okefenokee. Johnny Hickox has more recent ties to the swamp than Walker does: his father had been a swamp dweller and moonshiner. Hickox would prefer to live in the swamp, as independent as his father, but the law no longer permits such freedom.

We pushed off from Cowhouse before dawn, slipping along the neat, narrow channels of the park's boatways, which have been cut through the masses of shrubs flanking the southern shores of the island. There are few cypresses in this area, and it gives no hint of the grandeur of the old cypress bays deeper inside the swamp. When we stopped paddling and drifted in an expanse of scarcely moving open water, utter stillness prevailed. Even our heartbeats seemed to slacken to the tempo of the water. Watching black water eddying a leaf in almost imperceptible slow motion, I felt slowed myself. There was no hurry.

Dawn flushed quickly into the shrubs around us. Some birds with vivid markings moved ahead of the canoe. They were prothonotary warblers, a species common in the swamp yet rare enough elsewhere in the world to bring bird watchers from all over to see them here. A sudden commotion ahead revealed a tall gray bird thrashing aloft, long-necked and long-legged—a sandhill crane taking off.

"That's one of the great things about the swamp," Walker said with satisfaction. "Each day there's something new. Now, take that sandhill. When I first went to work for the park in 1955, you just never saw a sandhill on this side of the swamp. They were usually down toward the canal. They've come up here because, all of a sudden, we've got a plant moving in here, the paintroot, and the cranes love its seeds." This colonization of new territory by the redroot, or paintroot, as it is also known, is just one of a thousand similar movements and rhythms that are constantly changing the face of the Okefenokee.

As we moved silently through choked masses of water-loving shrubs and vines, the hollies, the myrtles, the bayberries and smilax that smother the water roads of the northern swamp, I tried to imagine men hunting, fighting and killing in this territory. But it all seemed unbelievable, especially when we arrived at what Walker called "the most beautiful part of the swamp." Big Water, as it is called, is a place where the trees draw together and the waterway ducks into shadows. It is a grand six-mile stretch of narrow lake flanked by thick forest. As we moved through this 100-foot-wide gap in the forest, our voices resounded with a peculiar echo, as though we were speaking inside a cathedral.

"There ain't no way to catch a man in the Okefenokee, if he don't want to be caught," Hickox said, as if reading my thoughts. What army could hold such country? To master the swamp a person needed a lifetime of practice. The stranger had to face new challenges each day.

Hickox spoke again. "You kin just sit here," he said, "and listen to the swamp breathin'."

For a moment there was total quiet, then the snap of a stick breaking among the trees, the slither of claws as a nuthatch circled a cypress trunk. An osprey hovered overhead squawking at this invasion of its territory, then swung away to a visible nest bulking in a dead cypress.

With the light of the sun ahead of us, splashing onto vivid jumbles of neverwet leaves striving upward, armies of lily leaves, gatherings of maiden canes, every view was yellow and white with flowers. It was difficult now to recall my first view of the swamp when the cypresses, still in their winter sleep, had not yet put forth leaves. Now the brilliance of their new green topknots matched the bright greens at water level. Even the Spanish moss seemed to have changed its drab color slightly as it prepared for flowering.

We left Big Water; the boat trail narrowed and wound back and forth through an infinite variety of trees and glades and thickets. South of us lay Minnie's Lake, on the way to Billy's Island, but after another hour of paddling, we turned to the east and entered a labyrinth of unmarked waterways. This was the beginning of another open territory, Floyd's Prairie, which lay between us and Floyd's Island itself. Even Hickox could not be sure of the way here. "I ain't ever been lost," he said, repeating an old swamper's maxim, "but sometimes I've been pretty confused." He calculated that as long as we kept bearing southeast, we had to reach Floyd's Island. And he was right.

For four hours we ran into one dead end after another, but always found a branching trail that led us on another few hundred yards. Eventually we cut into a tourist boat trail that led west toward the main route south to Billy's Island. We reached Floyd's Island in the late afternoon. At this island, about four miles long and less than a mile wide, we drove in the canoe and set out to portage through the thick pines to a spot where Walker and Hickox knew we could spend the night.

When we finally came to our camping ground there was a fairy-tale unreality about it. Nestled among giant magnolias and oaks was a cabin. At first glance it appeared perfect—shingled, windowed and porched —and seemingly waiting for the wilderness traveler to step inside it. But as I headed for its front door Hickox cautioned me. "Careful," he said, "the rattlers sometimes stay inside."

We bedded down to the sound of distant crashing—bears moving across the island—and I lay thinking about the past of this place. Dan Hebard, the head of a large lumber company, had so loved hunting in the swamp—of which he then owned a large part—that he had built this cabin so he could live and hunt in the Okefenokee as much as he pleased. In the early light of next morning the cabin, though a little more weather-beaten than it had appeared in the gloom of the previous evening, was still extraordinary—solid cypress wood from rooftop to foundation, its shingles and walls and floors as perfect as the day they were made some 60 years ago. "Used to be full of cypress furniture too," Hickox said, "but that's all been stolen years ago."

We left Floyd's Island and paddled through a long, narrow waterway that the refuge people had dynamited through the thickets of shrubs and trees. As we came out of this veritable tunnel, open country spread before us, punctuated with cypresses and smoothed with a carpet of grasses undulating like silk under the suddenly rising sun.

"Chase Prairie," Hickox said. As he spoke, we saw a large alligator lying in the sun, her back covered with youngsters, their pretty markings dancing in reflected light. "Let's move," Hickox said, and the paddles dug deeply together. Alligators are normally dangerous only when they are prevented from reaching their nests or refuges, but their individual temperaments are as variable as those of any animal.

We had been moving east, but now we turned to travel due south. Ahead a frieze of trees appeared, and in a few minutes we paddled through a narrow opening in them and came out into the Suwannee Canal. This folly of the human imagination had been built to drain the entire swamp, to destroy all its forests, exploit its turpentine and reduce its morass to farming land. But on the ground, as from the air, it is still a magnificent sight, a water highway diminishing into a blue distance of trees. Egrets burst into view from nearby prairies, ospreys paused overhead and herons marked straight lines across the canal. A nearby tree was filled with a score of silent, watching vultures.

We had intersected the canal about halfway along its length, but instead of heading east toward the swamp entrance there, we doubled back west toward the terminus of the canal. Actually, the canal has no single terminus since it branches and rebranches in many places. We passed one branch so choked with plants that no water showed anywhere. We pushed on to another branch and headed down it. The feeling of plants pressing in on us was a palpable thing now. "Won't be many years before this one's blocked too," Walker said.

Our journey became a diorama of the wild overcoming the tame. The number of fallen trees increased, great pencils of wood slanted diagonally across our path, and the swarm of floating water plants expanded. Eventually we came to the abrupt end of the canal's main channel and a barrier of trees and shrubs. We stopped paddling, but the canoe did not stop. It swiveled, caught in eddying waters that propelled it inexorably toward a narrow channel that disappeared into the trees. This was our route to Billy's Island.

After an hour of fighting through vines, fallen trees and masses of vegetation, we came into more open country. The channel widened. Now it was heading with increasing speed toward its union with the Suwannee River waters near Billy's Island. In another half hour the canoe

Two generations of descendants of Dan Lee, one of the first white settlers in the Okefenokee in the 1850s, sit for a family portrait in 1913, surrounded by trophies of the hunt: the skins of a deer, a bear, a skunk and six raccoons. The Lees sold such skins to add to their scanty farm income.

slid into deep shade and drove up a shelving shore. Ahead, lined up like man-made poles, the slash pines disappeared away into sun and shadow. This was a new world of dry land; cypresses flanked the island, but the pines were dominant.

For a moment absolute, penetrating silence reigned, as if the island were holding its breath and waiting for us to land. "Hot damn," Walker said. "I don't care how many times I see it, this sure is a pretty place."

Being a Northerner, I expected ruins, foundations, mounds, marks of the hundreds of men who had been here. Instead, we walked through a solitude of nothing but wilderness. If there was an immediate sign of humanity's works, it was a well-spaced group of beautiful loblolly pines that had colonized the big field that old Dan Lee had cleared of slash pines. "This is where they plowed," Hickox said. "This is where they built the town." Walker picked up a two-foot section of railroad track.

Nearby, a giant live oak towered. "Old Lee would've built the first house right here," Hickox said. Of course, in this sandy ground nobody dug foundations. The Lee family home, the sawmill town with its theater, its dance hall, its stores, and its foundry and machine shop had sat lightly on this ground.

Hickox walked over into a deeply shaded place where a large square box loomed in rusty isolation. It was a steam boiler, rotted away to meaningless junk. "My daddy stoked this thing," Hickox said. He prowled around finding pieces of wire rope, lengths of twisted rods that had once held wooden water tanks together, the cast-iron wellhead pipe that had once supplied the town with water.

Even the Lee cemetery, on the northern side of the clearing, did little to bring back man's presence on the island. Some of the headstones reported short lives. "Pneumonia killed 'em early," Hickox said. "Don't forget the cholera, either," Walker added. One headstone was that of a youngster, James Henry Lee, who had been run over in 1924 by a log-train locomotive, an ironic ending for a wilderness boy.

Some 35 years after Dan Lee had settled Billy's Island, another white man had focused his eyes on the swamp, obsessed by a manic vision. It is doubtful whether anyone has ever studied the Okefenokee with the compulsive single-mindedness of Captain Harry Jackson. As his knowledge of the swamp grew, he became convinced that he could drain it, a project on which he was prepared to stake his fortune and those of other men. It was Jackson who formed the Suwannee Canal Company, which in March 1889 bought 380 square miles of the Okefenokee from the State of Georgia for 26.5 cents an acre. The company in turn bought up a number of private holdings.

For men like Dan Lee, who had moved into what had seemed complete wilderness, unowned, uncared for, the canal company looked like an onrushing disaster. Few swampers held land deeds, and Lee and his family faced eviction if the canal turned out to be successful. In the fall of 1891, if he had taken his boat east from Billy's Island, he would have seen the beginning of the canal construction. For a wilderness man like Lee, the sight would have been stupefying. Large dredges, capable of gouging channels 45 feet wide and six feet deep, were at work. The steam engines operated 24 hours a day under sun and searchlight; and every day of digging advanced the company 44 feet toward Lee's home.

Before the swamp-draining began, one expert had estimated that it would take 300 miles of canals to empty the swamp completely. Digging at the rate of three miles a year, Jackson could not—before the money ran out—get his boats and machines within range of the cypresses that then blanketed much of the central swamp. Lee, listening to the distant rumble of the machines, could not know this. Jackson evidently sought to speed his project by setting his men to digging a drainage ditch that headed east to the St. Marys River. This was designed to cut through the ridge that is the swamp's eastern limit, and was to be used to get the logs out of the swamp and into the river, and eventually to carry all the water out of the swamp. By 1894 the ditch was almost completed. But already it was apparent that the Okefenokee was not responding to the technology and dreams of a 19th Century exploiter. An old black helper on one of the dredges summed up the dilemma when he asked, "If we's aimin' to put the water into the St. Marys, why is it all runnin' toward the Suwannee?"

Jackson died suddenly in 1895 and the canal-building stopped. He had dug 12 miles of canal and about six miles of drainage ditches. His dredges rotted and sank, or were burned by swampers. His steam engines were embraced by the teeming vegetation. A sawmill was looted and fell to pieces, and the tracks of his railroad were ripped up.

By the turn of the century the ownership of the swamp had passed to Northern lumbermen. The new owners—the Philadelphia-based Hebard Cypress Company—understood better than Jackson the difficulties of getting cypress out of the swamp; they were not possessed by the grandiosity of his vision. In 1909, a few years after old Dan Lee died, these pragmatic businessmen perched a railway track atop wooden piles, driving it 35 miles into the swamp. The railroad was serviced by

Workers at a 1913 logging operation in the swamp pause for their picture during a slack moment. The steam engine at right powered a mechanism known as an overhead skidder, used to lift logs onto flatcars. A moving cable ran from the top of the tree spar at rear right to a pulley in the woods at left. Attached to the cable was a boxlike trolley (center) to which cut logs were fastened and skidded across to the flatcar.

powerful locomotives pulling large flatcars loaded with great cypress logs. This time the engineering was adequate, the money sufficient, and the company prospered.

Since the Lee family had never held title to their land, there was no need to compensate them, but the company did give Lee's widow a $1,000 gratuity and let her stay in her house. By contemporary accounts she was not at all bitter, and some of her sons worked for the Hebard Company for years. The bitterness developed as newcomers poured in to take a look at these swamp "savages," as one man described them. Mrs. Lee was particularly incensed over a certain Dr. W. D. Funkhouser, who lectured on the Lees at the University of Kentucky in Louisville. He had explored the swamp for 20 days before reaching Billy's Island and getting his first glimpse of the Lee family. "Here," he reported, "we found a family of persons who in many ways can be compared only to animals. It consisted of an old, old woman, her three sons and two daughters, who had intermarried, and their eleven children. All of them were degenerate weaklings, undernourished, and had hookworm and bad blood, as the tests we made showed. . . . The family had no shelter except a rude lean-to built against a tree, and wore no covering to speak of, the children being entirely naked. While they spoke English, we had much difficulty in understanding them, as their vocabulary was Chaucerian, Spenserian, and Shakespearian."

Funkhouser conceded that these primitives had highly acute natural senses, comparable with those of animals. He said that they could smell the position of a rattler and that they trailed their prey like dogs, following the scent; they could describe almost every animal and insect in the swamp and "knew more about nature than anyone in our party."

Old Mrs. Lee had to put up with a lot more than visits by Funkhousers. She lived to see a hotel and a large store erected near her cabin. Some 600 people poured onto the island and telephone connection with the mainland was established. There was regular travel to and from the island by a railroad built on trestles. There were church meetings and a schoolhouse where, one writer observed, "the boys and girls are taught cracker English instead of Chaucerian English." Mrs. Lee lived to see a three-times-a-week motion-picture show on her husband's island.

Including lumbermen, swampers, turpentiners and hunters, there were more than 2,000 exploiters at work in this heyday of the swamp's destruction. More trestles were built and rail tracks fanned out, 200 miles long, in pursuit of the cypress. The roadbeds of the tramways, as

they were called, were so uneven that entire trains loaded with logs often were tipped into the water. Then the rescue engine and its large steam crane would go tearing off from Billy's Island, and the rescue team would work around the clock to get the flatcars back on the tracks, to dismantle the locomotive of its water tank, its boiler and its frame, and reassemble it.

Some of the swampers held to the hope that the Okefenokee would outlast the lumbermen and their works. Jackson Lee, one of Dan Lee's sons, was one of the optimists. He had been born on Billy's Island and had raised his family there. He was determined to outstay the locomotive and the ax. By 1925 the largest concentrated stands of timber had gone. By 1927 one historian was writing that "within a few more months this busy island will again, no doubt, slip back to the primitive; the scream of the locomotive will again be supplanted by the scream of the panther and the bobcat."

And so it was. Jackson Lee watched the boomtown turn into a ghost town. He remained on the island, living the life his father had trained him to enjoy. It stuck in my mind that Jackson Lee's best memory of his home, before the arrival of the lumbermen and the city people, was not that he was poverty stricken and ill educated and out of touch with the real world. It was simply that his family was self-sufficient.

He remembered how his wife would go to the water's edge and catch a frog to use for bait to catch a fish that she would cut up for larger bait to catch a basketful of large fish for supper. Jackson kept hogs and cows and worked a garden. He made his own cornmeal and grits. He knew how to catch a raccoon; he had become expert at killing alligators before he was a teenager; it was easy to get a deer in those days. The great thing about wilderness life, he said, was that "you didn't particularly need very much money."

The Okefenokee was without doubt the most accessible wilderness left to man on the North American continent at that time, and Jackson Lee was trying to make a simple statement about the quality of his life in such conditions. But even the Lees were beaten in the end, ironically by forces mobilizing to preserve the wilderness they had seen threatened by the lumbermen. The federal government took over much of the Okefenokee as a wildlife refuge. In 1937 Dan Lee's grandson, Harrison Lee, was ordered to leave. He was the last man to live on the island with his family. He was forced to go into a world dominated by the Depression. Life had been beautifully simple on Billy's Island, where all a man needed to survive was a pole, a punt, a knife and a spear. But that was gone forever, and so was much of the rest of wilderness America.

Although Walker and Hickox and I walked for an hour through a changeless serenity of pines, the only other signs of man were in the part of town once occupied by blacks, where old pots and pans were strewn around and lines of fallen brick fireplaces indicated rows of vanished shanties. We sat, our backs against pines, and the island stirred around us. Thrushes walked at our feet. Jays hammered nuts to pieces high overhead. Woodpecker cries bounced among the trees with cave-like echoes. Mockingbirds, towhees, wrens and squirrels darted from pine-needled earth to tendrils of moss caught in pine topknots.

A hundred feet away a cat came into sight in one smooth bound and faced us, motionless. I had never seen a bobcat and this first view was a long one as he considered our intrusion of his island. Then, in the instant that my eyes flicked upward to catch a glimpse of a great blue heron, the cat was gone.

I got up and stretched my legs. In this wild paradise of pines, this hauntingly peaceful place, it was hard to imagine the hoots of locomotive whistles sharing the air with the screams of surviving cougars and the howls of Florida wolves. To this island of 100-foot-high pines John Hickox' father had brought his 18-foot punt loaded with 30 gallons of Saturday-night revelry for the lumbermen. Pistol shots, lynchings, murders and fights had marked the advent and disappearance of civilization. I was looking at a wilderness that had outlasted its exploiters—and its benign human inhabitants as well.

As we reluctantly pushed the canoe back out into Billy's Lake, an evening breeze whispering in the pine tops, nobody spoke. Each of us came from a totally different background, but each had the same thought. Each of us wanted to possess that island for himself, or be possessed by it. The day's journey had been an instruction in the durability of this wilderness. Given half a chance, it wins in the end—just as old Billy Bowlegs had triumphed—because it is a correct state of nature.

The Greening of Billy's Island

PHOTOGRAPHS BY WOLF VON DEM BUSSCHE

An old Creek Indian legend tells of an island Eden that some lost and weary hunters stumbled on long ago in the Okefenokee Swamp. A band of beautiful Indian women feasted them with oranges, dates and corn cakes, and sent them on their way refreshed. The hunters' fellow tribesmen, obsessed with the tale, tried over and over to locate the island but were never able to find it again; it seemed to have disappeared in the mysterious reaches of the swamp.

There is a similar note of a lost civilization in the story of Billy's Island, a four-by-two-mile patch of land lying near the center of the Okefenokee. It is full of surprises, for lodged among the thriving pines and grasses are assorted artifacts, such as the engine boiler shown opposite, that strongly hint of a peopled past in the history of the island.

The island's name goes back to days even earlier than its moldering monuments, to a legendary Seminole Indian named Billy Bowlegs who lived there with his tribe in the late 18th and early 19th centuries. Billy made friends with the white man, emulated his ways and learned to speak his language.

The boiler—along with the other rusty bits of ironmongery shown on the following pages—is a remnant of a century later. In 1909 the Hebard Lumber Company of Philadelphia set up operations in the swamp to cut its rich growth of timber, and established headquarters on Billy's Island. In the next few years a town grew up and acquired a population of 600. The settlement eventually included a church, a school, a general store, telephone wires and railroad tracks, a smithy, a liquor still, a movie house, a baseball diamond and a boardinghouse where a bed and meals could be had for $5.50 per week. From this base the company's hired hands went out into the surrounding swamp and took a billion board feet of timber—cypress, bay, gum and other kinds.

After 18 years, the timber ran out and the operation ended in 1927. The company tore down the small buildings and shipped the large ones elsewhere by rail, leaving behind only the rusting relics that are now lying about the island. In the years since then nature has reclaimed its site. Pines, sycamores, wax myrtles and various kinds of tall grasses have shot up everywhere around the ironmongery, and detritus left by man is disintegrating and blending into the landscape.

A boiler that once served a steam engine recalls the human enterprise that throbbed in the early 1900s on Billy's Island—now thick again with pine, live-oak and laurel-oak trees.

A steam-engine boiler—remnant of an old locomotive—corrodes among slash pines, the dominant growth in a forest reclaiming itself.

Three washtubs, nested one inside the other, lie amid resurgent pine, scrub oak and grasses.

Tall grass advances on a kitchen stove that was once labored over by a boardinghouse cook.

In a clearing that is fringed by a spreading stand of pines and scrub oak, a derelict truck frame is cushioned by twigs and dead leaves.

Steam-boiler pipes now resemble nature's detritus; they look as though they were fallen tree saplings.

Cypress logs—cut at the island's shore and hauled inland to this site for reasons now forgotten—are encircled by healthy young pines. Their bark gone and their exposed wood worn smooth by the elements, the logs in time will contribute their own nutriments to the forest's growth.

4/ The Haunt of the Ivorybill

I have visited the favorite resort of the Ivory-Billed Woodpecker, those deep morasses...which seem to admonish intruding man to pause and reflect on the many difficulties ahead. JOHN JAMES AUDUBON/ ORNITHOLOGICAL BIOGRAPHY

One summer evening in 1946 a swamper named Will Cox was poling along Big Water—the narrow lake in the north-central part of the swamp—when he saw an ivory-billed woodpecker clinging to a limb of a big cypress. The sun was low behind his back and its light struck the woodpecker and illuminated its white bill with exceptional clarity. More than a quarter of a century later Uncle Will, past his 75th birthday and one of the oldest of the swamp dwellers, remembered the sight vividly. "Looked just like ivory," he told me. "Real bright and clear. No mistakin' what it was."

Uncle Will was one of the last men in the swamp to see an ivorybill, a woodpecker that has haunted the Okefenokee like a will-o'-the-wisp for the past 100 years. There is no doubt that the ivorybill possessed a special quality. To early swamp travelers, seeing it was the reward for hard journeying into the most remote fastnesses of the swamp. An aura attached itself to the elusive, unpredictable bird, fostered by its strikingly white and shiny bill, its showy color, its utterly distinctive cries and its unusually large size for a woodpecker. Unlike the common pileated species, it did not tolerate the arrival of men and fled from their presence when its special world was destroyed by them.

"They used to nest in big cypress timber," Uncle Will recalled. "A lot of that big cypress timber had holes. And then, as it was being cut out, of course they'd move . . . and they finally left."

The flaming red crest of the male (the female's was black), the stark white beak ("flashes like sun shinin' through crystal," in one description), the large, white wing patches against the gleaming black body, the white stripes running from below the eye down the side of the neck to meet in the middle of the back, all combined to set the ivorybill apart. In flight it looked like a pair of black-and-white flags being waved steadily in the air.

Its voice also separated it from other woodpeckers, but no one can quite agree about its calls. The ornithologist A. A. Allen got the one extant recording of the ivorybill's voice in the 1930s when he tracked down a pair in Louisiana. Apparently the ivorybills hunted in pairs, communicating constantly, and Allen's recording sounds like a series of muted trumpet notes tooted on a single pitch. But there was another, louder cry that John James Audubon heard and described as "the high, false note of a clarinet."

The ivorybill was never common, apparently because it had developed an ecological niche of its own as an exploiter of trees that had been killed or sickened by attacks of drought, fire or the flat-headed, wood-boring beetle. In its search for this insect, one of its favorite foods, the ivorybill could strip nearly all the bark off a stricken tree. But the large-scale destruction of Southern forests wiped out the magnificent stands of hardwoods in which the bird thrived.

It is unlikely that the ivorybill survives today in the swamp, though a few pairs may lurk in the trackless wilderness of the central-western Okefenokee. There Minnie's Island and Camp Island, protected by impenetrable thickets of cypress and shrubs and by a morass of peat, remain beyond the reach of boatmen and of any but the most determined walkers. In June 1912, a team of biologists from Cornell University led by Albert H. Wright, making what they called "a biological reconnaissance" of the swamp, walked through this ivorybill country. Travel became ferociously difficult and the men decided to camp at the base of a large dead pine, surrounded by one of the worst tangles of vegetation that any of them had ever seen. They were a little cheered while they were cooking supper to hear a pair of pileated woodpeckers, often mistaken for ivorybills though their beaks are horn colored, not white. They neither saw nor heard an ivorybill, but they awoke early the next morning to a symphony of bird song: the quick scolding of white-eyed vireos expressing their irritation at intruders; the whistling of Swainson's warblers; the gentle singing of the hooded warbler and the parula warbler; the cries of tufted titmice, friendly birds with crests sweeping back from their gray heads; and the nervous calls of the ceaselessly active Carolina wrens. The background to all this bird song was the slow, hollow knocking of pileated woodpeckers.

The men heard, too, the prothonotary warbler, for whom bird watchers still visit the swamp, since it is predictably there except in the winter when it migrates to Central America. The prothonotary is so spectacular a bird, its plumage so exquisite, that it forces you to pay attention when it is around. Its head, neck and underparts are a sparkling gold, softening to a paler shade on the belly. The greenish-yellow color of the back changes to bluish gray at the rump, and the wings and tail are silvery. In flight this bird seems like a small sun broken away from the parent sun that flames above it. I have seen it perched in trees that curved down to the water in the swamp and flashing its bright colors across open prairies. It is the only eastern warbler to nest in tree cavities; old woodpecker holes are its favorites. Wright and his team were understandably delighted to find it in the Okefenokee. Perhaps it made their physical discomfort easier to bear. As it was, they took more than two weeks to travel about 20 miles. They fell frequently or sank into sphagnum coverings, nearly broke their ribs on submerged cypress knees, and had to pull one another from trembling-earth bogs.

In such country the ivorybill might long remain elusive. When I flew over its last-known Okefenokee stronghold on Minnie's Island there was no sign of a deer track, a watercourse or any distinctive groups of pines or cypresses to guide the traveler through the bird's territory. By plane from the small airport at Waycross it is only a 10-minute flight to Big Water and two minutes from there to Minnie's Island. On foot, because of the peculiar difficulties of travel in this part of the Okefenokee, no one really knows how long the journey would take. Normally I could walk through sphagnous bog and shallow prairie at a maximum speed of one foot per second, or 3,600 feet—less than three quarters of a mile—per hour. But this was top speed, without resting or without meeting unexpectedly deep bogs or impregnable thickets. In fact, only about 45 minutes of travel was possible for me every hour; the need for frequent rest brought down my speed to 2,000 feet, or about one third of a mile, an hour. The old swampers could walk the full length of the swamp—about 35 miles—in about eight days, but they were able to do so only because of their intimate knowledge of all the terrain, and their extraordinary strength and endurance. I knew I could never reach Minnie's Island on foot. Yet each time I passed along the north-south boat

On the alert for both prey and danger, a great blue heron watches from its post in a tangle of grasses and shrubs. With a wingspan of five to six feet, this kind of heron is the second largest of the 233 species of birds in the Okefenokee, exceeded in size only by the red-headed sandhill crane.

trail of Big Water, the dusky cypresses curtained a stage of mystery. If the curtain could be raised, the shadows suggested, another part of the swamp might be revealed. This was not just my own reaction. Most swamp travelers, even men who have lived there all their lives, feel this pull. However, the moods and thinking that the Okefenokee inspires are not always rational.

One morning in high summer I paddled my canoe into a cluster of cypress knees along Big Water, got out and walked west through the trees. For two hours I worked through the unique domain created by the cypresses growing in shallow, puddled water, the cylindrical protuberances of their knees so thick in places it was difficult to walk through them. The cries of distant birds sounded artificial, transformed by passage through the almost sepulchral hush of the trees. The ivory-bill existed powerfully in my head. Its cries echoed in my inner ear: tiny horns rapidly repeating one note. In a wilderness dominated by primeval sounds, their voices must have seemed an imitation of sounds made by men. Perhaps that was one of the reasons they were remembered with such clarity.

Minnie's Island lay three miles ahead of me to the west. When I came out of the cypresses I faced a prairie. Its vastness, after the constriction of the forest, expanded before me. Beyond it, I knew, was another prairie, then a bogland, and beyond that another prairie, another bog. The open water of the prairie in front of me, still patched with floating leaves, swarmed with wheeling forms. For a second I thought these must be fish chasing each other at the surface. Then I realized I was seeing the reflections of soaring birds.

When one travels through the swamp by the conventional waterways, the birds are generally invisible except in the more open reaches of the eastern swamp. To find birds in other parts of the Okefenokee, it is necessary to walk the islands, to work through the sphagnous wastes, to trudge through the cypress bays and the tree houses—the wooded islands that form out of the peat. It is then that the birds come to the human watcher. As I looked across the prairie it appeared that several hundred wood ibises had found an updraft and were turning and twisting in a towering column of life. These large water birds, the only species of stork native to North America, had never before struck me as joyful creatures. But this most certainly was flying for its own sake, necks and wings and legs fully outstretched. The wings, spreading about five feet, black rimmed at the back, and the black tail feathers emphasized the beauty of the off-white bodies in flight.

The precision with which the wood ibises kept their columnar formation eventually tempted me to wade into the prairie so that I came under the chimney of their flight. I looked up into its empty interior while the birds circled its walls, catching the sun. Their mood appeared to be infectious. A score of anhingas quick-flapped back and forth through and around the base of the flight chimney. Then, after a while, the wood ibises came gliding silently to earth and lost themselves in the vastness of the prairie.

More plebeian birds immediately announced themselves. From several thickets and nearby cypress houses came the yowling of the ubiquitous catbird, the gray, black-capped sentinel of the bogland, alert for any intruder. A brown thrasher, another common swamp bird, bolted out of a holly bush and vanished; naturally suspicious, it had no desire to wait around until I sloshed back to the fringes of the prairie. Blue jays rocketed overhead, their rowdy screeches berating my presence. A pinewoods sparrow appeared suddenly on the top of a wax-myrtle bush, chanted its brief, cheerful song and disappeared. A mockingbird silently inspected me from a dead cypress. Far distant but also watching, a red-shouldered hawk screamed—if such a scratchy, chicken-like squawk can be called screaming. What had seemed an empty and desolate wilderness was full of life.

The birds of the swamp can be very dramatic in their movements. Some, for example, prefer to feed beyond the swamp's borders despite the ample wilderness larder it offers. The red-winged blackbird, while it enjoys the bonnet worms that live in the stems of swamp water lilies, prefers the grain that it finds in the fields of farms beyond the Okefenokee. As a result, red-winged blackbirds may be seen passing overhead in the thousands on morning flights out of the swamp and evening flights back in. The mass movements of various other bird species are equally memorable in the seasonal migrations that go on constantly at a steady ebb and flow. Now, in summer, many birds had left the swamp for the North. Most of the warblers had evacuated—some, like the yellow-rumped warblers, leaving in visible waves.

The appearances and disappearances of the birds are often seemingly abrupt, adding to the swamp's sharp changes of mood. Hundreds of robins may be seen in the trees of a single island one day, and not be seen there again until they return from flights to New England, Quebec, Newfoundland and even Labrador. And when migrants leave for the North, immigrants swarm in from Florida, including thousands of ibis-

Gregarious white ibises, the most common wading birds in the swamp, share a rookery near its western edge. A white ibis will return to the same rookery night after night, no matter how far it ranges during the day in search of food.

es and egrets and herons that habitually summer in the Okefenokee.

One group of birds reside in the swamp except in summer, when they migrate north to breed. They are no different from the birds you might expect to see almost anywhere in the South in the fall, winter and spring: pied-billed grebes, kestrels, American coots, common snipe, ruby-crowned kinglets, white-throated sparrows, swamp sparrows and song sparrows.

Another group of birds leave the swamp during the winter, some off on short journeys down the Florida peninsula in search of slightly warmer weather or better hunting, others bound for Central and South America on really long migrations. The green heron and the cattle egret filter down into Florida. The yellow-billed cuckoo takes off for South America. The eastern kingbird goes to Florida while the eastern wood peewee migrates to Central America. The white-eyed vireo flies down the Gulf Coast to Yucatán and South America.

Some birds do not leave the swamp at all. Oddly, most of the resident birds are not water birds. These are outnumbered by common birds also seen almost everywhere outside the swamp. Thus, on the pine barrens and pine island fringes, the visible birds include blue jays, tufted titmice, mockingbirds, catbirds, brown thrashers, loggerhead shrikes, red-winged blackbirds, cardinals, Carolina wrens, barred owls, bobwhites, red-shouldered hawks, ground doves and mourning doves. In the trees, woodpeckers are almost always visible, the most common being the downy, followed by the pileated, the common flicker, the red-bellied woodpecker and, rarely, the red-cockaded woodpecker.

Of all the ducks in the Okefenokee, only the wood ducks remain there steadfastly throughout the year. In the winter they share the company of mallards and black ducks, green-winged teal and American wigeon. During the nonsummer months, as many as 10,000 of these birds may inhabit the swamp. I had caught glimpses of the ducks on early visits to the prairies along the eastern side of the swamp, but by now they had gone almost en masse. And with them had gone the woodcock and the snipe, the shore birds that fly into the swamp from New England.

Slogging westward across the prairie, I reached a cypress house and made my way into its dark, thickly wooded interior. Instantly I was smothered in a swarm of mosquitoes. Everywhere in the swamp the mosquitoes spring up in pockets, millions thick in places, with devastating effect. I had to shield mouth and nose against them, and I could feel hundreds of them forcing their way down my collar line, up my sleeves, biting through shirt and trousers, in my hair and ears. Because there is no escape, you have to learn stoic acceptance of the bites. I waded forward. A choked cry came from the house. A beautiful pileated woodpecker lay on its back in a small pool, in the last few minutes of dying of disease or old age. It bore no sign of injury.

Beyond the house a score of red-winged blackbirds gathered in silent congregation, darted away and dropped down to snatch at some insect food, many of them landing on lily pads and dashing from one floating plant to another. Far across the prairie a laugh sounded. It seemed derisive, and perhaps it was—mocking my attempts to invoke extinct ivory-billed woodpeckers here, a king rail was making an unaccustomed daylight call. I knew I would not see this bird that sounded so amused at my floundering progress through the swamp. The king rail, usually most active at dusk and dawn, skulks in long grasses the rest of the time, defending its privacy against intruders by hiding or running off. It rarely flies, and as a result its wings are weak. When it is forced to take to the air, its legs, so long and strong on the ground, hang limply as all its effort goes into a short, clumsy, defensive flight.

The mosquitoes, the heat and the enveloping sweat were all enough to quell my enthusiasm for bird watching. But the birds of the swamp are capable of calling attention to themselves in their unexpected ways of moving. Ahead of me the graceful white forms of egrets assumed a variety of poses, necks angled as they walked deliberately through shallow waters. A great blue heron stood in majestic solitude in the middle of a patch of bog. Three white ibises bunched together, their black-tipped wings stroking in unison and their necks outstretched, passed over the prairie in rapid flight. Turkey vultures circled and black vultures winged along a line of distant cypresses. The turkey vultures, their heads and the bare skin of their necks a bright red, soared in graceful spirals, broad wings outstretched. The black vultures, their necks and heads ebony colored, were far less graceful, the effort of flight more apparent. Though they are heavier than the turkey vultures, their wings are shorter and they must flap them more frequently to stay aloft. But in a fight between these scavengers over food, the black vulture's extra weight and greater aggressiveness usually help it to settle the dispute in its favor.

Toward dusk, I knew, many of the water birds I was now seeing on this prairie would be taking off and heading for their rookeries along the eastern edge of the swamp, places of endless uproar and screech and clatter, especially in summer when fledglings in rough-stick nests are demanding to be fed. But evening was still to come, and the view ahead of me spoke of leisured, unhurried hunting in an expansive natural world. I stood and surveyed the scene until finally I could stand the mosquitoes no longer. When I saw some wood ducks, one of them trailing a line of ducklings, floating in a clear patch of water about 200 yards away, I decided to slip into the water. It was hot at the surface, deliciously cool at the bottom, and at least a partial refuge from the mosquitoes. I dropped to my knees and crawled along the shallows. The ducks I glimpsed through gaps in the weeds did not see me. I had gone about 100 yards toward them when, without warning, a series of spine-tingling bugle notes smashed the heavy air. A nearby cypress house that had appeared deserted had hidden a solitary sandhill crane. This tall, statuesque bird is the sentinel of the prairies just as the catbird is the alarmist of the boglands. Its five-foot height enables it to see over most of the prairie grasses and thickets and thus spot the approach of danger while there is still time to escape. The big dark bird curved away from the prairie and disappeared, its bugle calls fading. The diminishing sound, changing its tones as it went, combined with the graceful movements of the dark body against the green foliage to produce a memorable moment for me.

The voice of the sandhill crane is a match for the roaring of the alligator, not in the primeval sense, but in sheer exuberance. The cry is often sounded for no other reason than pure pleasure. Johnny Hickox, who had often listened to sandhill cranes, once told me that the old swampers had never accepted the scientific identification of these birds. "They got quite mad," he said. "To the swamper, those were whooping cranes, and no outsider was ever going to tell them different." I could not now argue with them, though I knew that the whooping crane is white, while the sandhill is gray; the whooping crane, almost a foot taller, is a more magnificent bird altogether. In any event, the swampers believed that the crane could communicate many different messages to other birds. They may have been right. In the wake of the sandhill's call, alarmed cries sounded all around me. Catbirds yowled, a mockingbird screeched and jays screamed. And the wood ducks I had been trailing were, of course, gone.

The swampers clung to another belief about the sandhill. They were convinced that the bird was totally monogamous—which is true as long as both mates live—but they also believed that if the female were killed the male became "an outcast for life." The swampers would shoot a

Its brow a bright red, a fleet-footed gallinule trips as lightly across lily pads as if it were walking on the water. This bird is capable of a superb balancing act. It will occasionally stop and use its beak to grasp and turn up the edge of a pad; then, standing on this unstable platform with the aid of its long toes, it will eat the insects clinging to the underside of the leaf.

crane at its nesting place, then watch as the mate of the slain bird circled the nesting area for days after the killing. The "mourning" of the crane affected them but this did not stop the shooting. The crane was good eating in itself; besides, the swampers were certain, it warned off the ducks they hunted, and that was serious, because ducks were a staple food for them.

Beyond the value of the ducks as provender, the swampers appreciated the natural drama of their autumnal migrations, and they thought it was possible to gauge what kind of winter was coming by the number of ducks arriving in the swamp: an abundance of ducks meant a cold winter to come.

For me, at this point, images of the autumn and winter to come were very remote. The air had become almost unbearably oppressive. The sun was haloed in orange haze, the color of the light permeating the prairie. In the sky ahead, over a section of the prairie that narrowed into a long reach of water flanked by young cypresses, a large bird with a long neck flew along, beating its wings rapidly, gliding, beating again, the pattern of the black-and-white body clearly visible. Then it turned abruptly and dived vertically, throwing up a spout of water and green leaves and one desperately leaping fish.

In other times this bird was called a water turkey, and it is still so called today by some of the old swampers. The term better describes it than its Latin name, anhinga, though anhingas and true turkeys belong to totally different branches of the bird clan and though turkeys are not nearly the skillful fliers that anhingas are. But water turkey is an apt name because it suggests a bird that in its evolution has moved from the woods into the water. In former days, both wild turkeys—which are still found in the swamp—and water turkeys might loft into the tops of trees together. But the water turkey, its neck writhing (hence another name for it, snake-bird), could be a submarine one moment later. I knew that the bird I had just seen in a steep dive was whisking through the water at high speed, threading deftly through the tangle of water weeds, somehow able to see in water so gloomy and brown that when I lifted one lily leaf I could not see more than a few inches down. Although its feathers get wet because it lacks the protective oil glands of waterfowl, the anhinga has adapted to underwater swimming by developing solid bones that allow it to stay submerged. As I watched, the bird surfaced among some lilies with only its neck stuck up out of the water, in periscope fashion. The periscope shot quickly to another position, disappeared for half a minute, then reappeared among the cypresses. Now the bird held a small fish, and bird and fish took off like a tiny Polaris missile launching itself explosively from the water.

A sudden violent gust of hot wind, the appearance of dark clouds from the southeast and the abrupt disappearance of the sun sent me hastening back to the shelter of a cypress house. I was only 50 miles from the Atlantic and so within range of collisions of air moving between cool sea and hot land mass. To the east rain was already falling. Lightning danced and the opaque horizon grumbled with suppressed sound. The egrets and ibises and herons had all taken off. I presumed they intended to flank the storm in their return to their rookeries.

The rain approached the house as a solid gray wall and its hiss as it struck was the sound of an army of serpents. The onset of this storm was more than mildly disturbing. As was my custom, I had tied ribbons on vegetation to guide me back to Big Water, but they would be invisible in that murk of rain. The force of the storm struck the house and blotted out everything.

The summer rains of the Okefenokee, at their heaviest, are violent and frightening, suggesting the tropics. The cypress trunks around me ran with water. With the rain came a steady hail of debris, pieces of Spanish moss, small branches, a young bird beating its wings frantically against the burdening rain. A nuthatch clung motionless to a trunk nearby while a stream of water poured from a hole above, dislodging the remains of an old woodpecker's nest.

The clash of thunder and the snap of breaking twigs went on for nearly an hour. The rain continued. But it was getting late and I was no swamper, capable of navigating the morass in the dark. I left the cypress house and plunged into the water again in the direction of my canoe, through a massive embrace of other cypresses caught in gloom. My passage through them was a desperation of misplaced footsteps, sudden falls and doubts about where I was heading.

In the last vestiges of light I found the canoe and poled out into Big Water. The swamp had become a black and menacing presence around me. This hostility of raw wilderness, where puny bipeds with misplaced dreams are not wanted, offers a perfect sanctuary for the ivorybill. If there are still ivorybills in there, they may be safe for a while.

5/ Prodigal Plants in a Wet World

Whoever has beheld the manifold charms of this paradise
of woods and waters, comes away fascinated and spellbound.
Its majestic pines and cypresses, its peaceful waterways
and lily-strewn prairies...should be safeguarded.

FRANCIS HARPER/ *A SOJOURN IN THE PRIMEVAL OKEFINOKEE*

My first impression of the Okefenokee, at winter's end, was of a stillness of leaves, a languor of cypresses and Spanish moss, a scattering of blossoms frozen into their settings. By late summer, I had difficulty remembering this static view. Over the months the swamp plants had acquired forceful, even aggressive personalities.

The prodigal growth in the Okefenokee modifies and arbitrates the life of everything else there. The plants are the very core of the swamp's wild beauty, the essence of all its many atmospheres. Without plants, there would be no swamp in the Okefenokee, only a crystal-clear lake.

Ironically enough, the man-made Suwannee Canal offers the most visible testimony to the power of the struggle among the plants for space and light, water and food. Along the canal's length there is a certain orderliness. The cypresses and slash pines on each bank, compressed onto the narrow ridge of muck dug from the channel 75 years ago, are drawn up like guards of honor. In places, wild irises discreetly touch the banks with purple. But in other places, as well as at the ends of the canal, where smaller channels split away from the main canal, chaos rules. Into those narrow waterways that have not been kept open by federal refuge men or, in season, by the boats of fishermen, innumerable trees have fallen, some to drown and die, others to root again. Mounded around them are masses of plant debris out of which shrubs sprout. These rarely used channels are choked with water plants and are quite impassable.

Variations of this theme are apparent everywhere in the Okefenokee. As if by some grand design, teeming hosts of plebeian grasses and sedges, shrubs and water plants grow almost without cease, filling in the swamp with the mass of their decaying bodies and so gradually transforming it into a cushiony bog, a bog that eons hence may evolve into the same sort of solid pinelands that now cover millions of acres adjacent to the Okefenokee in southern Georgia.

I encountered this process at work in an Okefenokee prairie one evening when I was returning from a canoe trip to Gannet Lake, the southernmost accessible point in the swamp. I found the narrow water trail filled with a pungent black mass. It completely blocked the canoe's path. Sprawling atop it, like little waifs, were white and yellow lilies and tiny-flowered spikes of neverwets, or golden clubs, that the black mass had thrust up in its own rise out of the water.

I stepped carefully out of the canoe and onto the stuff. My foot went clean through it. I lost my balance and fell, still half expecting some sort of support. But there was no support. I went into the muck like a matron into a mud bath. This was pure peat, a mass of organic matter that had risen from the bottom of the prairie to the watery surface. In rising, it had stranded all the aquatic plants floating above it. When I scrambled back into the canoe, I was black, glistening with what appeared to be the slimiest mud. But this peat resembled mud only superficially. When I sloshed some water on myself, it washed the black off completely; my clothes were hardly stained.

The floating patch of peat was the result of the constant, hidden work of the plants of the prairie, and represented one of the many stages in its eventual consolidation into something approaching dry land. Plant generations follow each other with such rapidity that the cycle of their life, death and decay—the process of rendering living matter back into protein, carbohydrates, phosphates and acids—goes on continuously. Gas—formed in quantity by the decay of sunken, dead vegetation and trapped under the peat—had gathered so thickly that it had lifted an entire chunk of the bottom material. Aptly, the swampers dubbed this phenomenon a blow-up. These gas-manufactured patches of floating peat are called batteries when they are large sized. Often they are 20 feet wide and 100 feet long, and the newly exposed material floats buoyantly enough to accept seeds and permit their germination almost immediately.

As summer began waning, I saw more peat patches on Sapling Prairie on the northwestern side of the swamp. They had broken off, drifted with the water currents, and lodged at the edges of the prairie. Some blow-ups of previous years, even though they now hosted grasses, herbs and young shrubs, were still afloat; the roots of the plants were not long or strong enough to anchor the patch to the bottom.

"You can get lost in here pretty easily," Johnny Hickox had said. I could well understand this, with channels closing, new ponds appearing and patches of peat rising, floating, coalescing and sinking. But only slowly did I grasp the significance of what I was seeing: the swamp's dynamic process of self-destruction. The blow-ups and batteries represented a kind of climax in plant activity; the crowding of vegetation into every available space prepared the ground for the invasion of new species of shrubs and grasses that could not thrive in muck and water. What had started as patches of free-floating peat were visible at various stages of development. Some of the peat islands were merely grassed, a place where waterfowl could stand and scan the open water around them. Others were covered with low shrubs—swamp-loving buttonbushes in particular, their little rounded heads of white flowers raised on slender stems. The most mature islands—the swampers called them houses when they were dry and firm enough to use as hunting campsites—were dotted with trees and on the verge of turning into the even larger cypress "bays," tracts of more than 20 acres. This process begins when the cypress seeds fall on the expanding house and germinate in the rich peat.

But until an island reaches the house stage, there is no guarantee whatever of its permanence. The vegetation may survive or it may not, if it becomes submerged too deeply underwater. A battery may thicken and stabilize itself, or it may not. Many sink before the plants are established or even before their seeds germinate. I walked on one island in the intermediate stage, when its fate was not yet determined, and felt this earth raft bending under my feet. It was a bit like walking across a velvet-covered pool. The few young plants that were trying to take hold leaned toward me as I stepped, their tips trembled, and the earth shook.

I suspect that the number and density of houses in a prairie are good clues to its age. Some of the older prairies, like remote Territory, are hedged in so thickly by hundreds of houses that they no longer contain the great open stretches of water that characterize the younger prairies

The eerie, extravagant drapery of Spanish moss (right), a familiar sight in the swamp, almost totally conceals a bald cypress and a red-leaved tupelo tree. In spite of the name, it is not a moss but an epiphyte—a plant that derives its food from the air and from rain water without damaging the host tree on which its seeds settle. Scaly hairs that cover the plant's long stems give it its gray color. In early spring it sprouts small green-yellow flowers (above) that bathe the surrounding area in a delicate scent.

—Sapling, for instance; instead, they are crisscrossed by a series of nar-
rowish channels. The younger prairies, by contrast, have hundreds of
acres of open water lightly patched with yellow bonnets and golden
neverwets; and the houses of cypress and pine are less densely packed.
But while these prairies can be traveled everywhere at high water, the
older prairies lead the voyager almost invariably into cul-de-sacs, or
into tortuous branching channels that quickly maroon him in a fea-
tureless prison of plants.

For me each prairie has its own distinctive atmosphere. I found Territory a mournful place; the narrowness of its waterways, its somber si-
lences bespeak sadness. Perhaps this is because Territory, already old,
suggests it is preparing for death. North of it Redbird Prairie, which is
unrecorded in swamp literature and difficult to reach except by heli-
copter, also has a foreboding look; though not as old as Territory, it
shows signs of aging in the almost continuous massing of its cypresses,
pines and understory brush.

Being wilderness, the swamp is never static. In the prairies, plants not
only may be stranded by the rising of the peat in which they are rooted, but they may dry out in the desiccating rays of the sun, or may be destroyed by fire. On the swamp's true islands, the remnants of the
sandbars of the Pleistocene Epoch, many trees are shallow rooted. Sudden violent storms may strike them down by the score. The winds
drive in from all points of the compass, and even in the hammocks
—those sturdy congregations of hardwood trees—the result may be an
indescribable confusion of smashed magnolia, hickory, live oak, water
oak and laurel oak that have flourished for more than a century.

Ordinarily, however, the hammocks—which occupy relatively high
points on swamp islands with less sandy soil—contain some of the Okefenokee's most durable plants and trees. The Indians used these sites
as burial mounds, and early swampers cleared and cultivated them.
Nearly all the islands once had hammocks, large or small; at one time a
hammock covered about a tenth of Chesser Island, and some islands
—Mixon's, Hickory, Craven—were actually called hammocks.

Because the hammocks built up humus they were the most attractive
parts of the swamp for human settlement; for years, until the federal
government banned unauthorized digging, they yielded up chunks of Indian pottery, arrowheads, beads and sea shells. Hammocks offered
superb campsites shaded against the blistering heat of the sun by dense
growths not only of oak, magnolia and hickory but of laurel, sweet

gum, holly, bay and other species. Some trees provided extra blessings.
Saw palmetto, the most common American palm, bears black fruit that
the Indians loved. The old swampers made heady wine from the grapes
of the wild muscadine vine, and used the evergreen leaves of the red
bay, a member of the laurel family, for a seasoning as aromatic as
those derived from some of its relatives—cinnamon and sassafras. The
acorns of the live oak, and the blackberries, gallberries and myrtle-
berries that grew on the hammocks or at their edges attracted mammals
and birds that were easy for the Indians and swampers to hunt.

The supreme trees of the Okefenokee are, of course, the cypresses.
They are everywhere and anywhere. In places they pack together in
massive congregations, but then peter out into a thin straggle of individual trees dotted for miles across the bogs and prairie fringes. Then,
unaccountably, they thicken again and form dense bays. They can grow
in sand above the visible water line, areas that typically are pine country, yet they also flourish in quagmire. Their rate of growth is steady,
about a foot a year, and this pace slows down only after a century.

Many cypresses are as old as 400 years, colossi towering as high as
120 feet. The tree's great resistance to decay—a quality that, along
with the handsome look of its lumber, attracted the early exploiters
—is perhaps the major secret of its survival, but not the only one.
Against hostile forces other than man the cypress can defend itself in a
variety of ways. To combat high winds, it spreads its roots widely and
deeply. It puts forth a canopy of foliage so thin that fire seldom gets
much sustenance from it. Lightning may strike and leave the trunk of
the tree riven, but the cypress responds to this insult by sending out
fresh sprouts from the jagged remains. It responds, according to local
swamp lore, even to the visits of birds. Some cypresses are bent horizontally, again bent upward, and bent and rebent again at right angles.
No one could explain this curiosity, I was told, until one day somebody
noticed that egrets and anhingas often broke off the growing leaders
when they perched on the tips of young cypresses. The tip would grow
sideways until it was able to grow upward again; even if it were re-
broken, the pattern of new growth would be repeated. Nothing could
stop that upward thrust toward the light and sun.

Contorted into innumerable shapes, the cypress is a study in stub-
born majesty, seemingly inviolable. The one other contender for
supremacy among the trees of the Okefenokee is the pine; so great is
the pine's capacity to colonize that stands of it may, in fact, eventually
replace stands of cypress. Like the cypress, the pine suffered for years

In a forest of slash pines the yellowish brown of cinnamon ferns offers a lively autumnal contrast to the green of saw palmettos. In spring and summer the cinnamon fern looks like many other green ferns, but in the fall it takes on the color that inspired its name.

at the hands of man. Initially its slender, soaring trunks made ideal masts and spars for sailing ships, and it also provided an incalculable bounty of naval stores—resin, pitch, tar, turpentine, pine oil. Later it went into the making of railroad ties and paper pulp. But again like the cypress, the pine has survived civilization's assaults on the swamp.

Two species predominate, both on the islands of the swamp and in the higher, drier ground of the adjoining pine barrens. One is the longleaf, whose leaves hang in tufts that look like coarse grass, and may be as much as 12 inches long. Growing as high as 100 feet on a relatively narrow trunk, the longleaf flourishes best in sandy soil. The slash pine prefers moist soil, often in close proximity to cypress bays and ponds. It is somewhat shorter than the longleaf, seldom reaching more than 80 feet in height, and is distinctive for the orange color of its branchlets and twigs. But its greatest distinction is one that also brought the slash pine its name. A slash, in Southern terminology, is an open area strewn with trees that have been felled by fire or storm or man; and the slash pine is so called because it is the first tree to get a foothold after such disasters. It is one of the fastest-growing of all Eastern forest trees, able in 20 years to grow a trunk six inches in diameter.

The plant world of the Okefenokee is multistoried, a fascination to the eye at every level. Carpeting the center of the swamp, and creeping inexorably in all directions, are the tangled, spindly, gray-green leaves of sphagnum moss, the chief component of peat bogs. Unlike most other mosses, sphagnum has empty, porous cells in its leaves that absorb and retain great amounts of water, many times its weight. Though it may appear thoroughly dry at the top, its matted underparts will release a trickle of water at the merest pressure. Sphagnum has thus made the heart of the Okefenokee, in effect, a giant sponge.

Omnipresent in the swamp whenever the eye looks upward is another plant that bears the name of moss, but in this instance incorrectly. Spanish moss is not a moss at all, nor is there anything Spanish about it. It is an epiphyte, a rootless plant that derives all the nutrients it needs from the air and rain. Spanish moss hangs deftly draped around the upper, middle and lower branches of trees as if master decorators had positioned it in place. To me it has always seemed a limp festoon of gray tendrils. Yet, for all its appearance of nonlife, it lives ingeniously. It absorbs rain and holds the moisture under a thick covering of scales. It can draw additional sustenance from its supporting tree's mineral-rich dead cells and flaking bark, washed down by the rain from the higher branches. But festoons of Spanish moss, eerily hanging by themselves on solitary dead twigs, with no tree or branch above them, do exist solely on substances from the air and rain.

Unlike other epiphytes, many of which actually attach themselves to trees and produce fruit, Spanish moss never becomes a part of the tree on which it hangs. It is completely self-contained, producing infinitesimally light seeds that float to new places of germination and sprout where they settle. When I looked at the moss close up, at the height of its growing season, I could detect what are termed flowers growing from the tiny gray extensions of some branches. But what flowers ever looked like dead shoots?

Between the carpet of sphagnum moss and the overhanging drapery of Spanish moss are assorted and often overlapping levels of the Okefenokee plant world, in many places so crowded and so varied that they defy any layman's attempt at an estimate of their number. One botanist told me that to learn most of the shrubs and herbs took three or four years of steady study. I was given the names of at least 30 different species of shrubby plants and more than 200 herbaceous plants. Some float; some crawl along the ground; some climb. Each has its special fascination, even for the most blasé of botanists: the alluring yellow jasmine, with its strychnine-like poison; the climbing heath, which can grow straight up beneath the dead bark of a pond cypress; the coral greenbriar, whose near-white berries turn a spectacular red in winter; the fragrant deer's tongue, whose leaves often end up in a tobacco mixture; the resurrection fern, more formally known as *Polypodium polypodioides,* which mostly grows on the limbs of live oaks and magnolia trees. For me, this species epitomizes the plant life of the swamp. During dry seasons, it dries up so thoroughly that it looks quite dead; but soon after a rain it assumes the bloom of bright green health.

Each plant finds its ideal habitat, and struggles to keep its place there. The competition for space and light and food is strongest along the edges of every lake and pond, of cypress bay and house, of island and canal, where jungles of aquatic plants mass. At such places the cinnamon fern seeks more growing room by poking its fronds daintily but persistently into a sea of carex, one of the Okefenokee's most prolific sedges. White water lilies take over where the water is shallow and the current mild; their relatives, the spatterdocks, whose flowers are yellow and cuplike, predominate in slightly deeper waters. Delicate duels for a share in the shallows are fought between chain ferns and maiden cane, a kind of grass that is related to the domesticated millet. The maiden cane is so thickly compacted that the swampers used to grab fistfuls of these tangles and haul them, like heavy Persian rugs, over the side and into their boats. Hiding in this matted vegetation were all kinds of small turtles, frogs, salamanders, fish, beetles and other bugs —superb bait for fishing.

Some members of the Okefenokee plant community have a specialized means of survival. These are the so-called meat-eaters, each with its own device for trapping and consuming insects. Studded along the fringes of islands and in the boggy shallows of the prairies are the sundews, which trap insects on leaves covered with sticky glands; in this way the sundews get the nutrients that are otherwise scarce in their world. Another species of meat-eater, the graceful pitcher plant, employs a different sort of snare: a hollow, parchment-like tube into which insects fall. Often the tube will contain a collection of doomed flies, moths and ants, prevented from leaving by the waxy, slippery inner surface of the tube.

Within the dense thickets that challenge the traveler everywhere in the Okefenokee, more shrubs and herbs abound. If the traveler happens also to be a word-collector, the names alone are seductive. How could I resist the swamp sweet spire, the soap bush, the hurrah bush? But it was one thing to be intrigued by the local terminology, another to identify each plant and try to make sense of its natural history. It is a confusing matter, to say the least. The swamp sweet spire, I learned, is actually a Virginia willow. The soap bush, also called lather leaf and poor man's soap, is actually a deciduous heath; I discovered for myself the reason for these names by rubbing the leaves between my hands in swamp water, and getting a foam that really cleaned. The name of the hurrah bush may indeed have derived from the swampers' use of it to hide their moonshine. But it sometimes masquerades under the name of fetterbush, which actually belongs to an entirely different shrub.

The herbs have equally enchanting names, such as lizard's tail, Indian turnip, fly poison, tiger tail and blue-eyed grass, and they are just as difficult to sort out as the shrubs. Even botanists argue among themselves in identifying some of them. The blue-eyed grass is actually an iris, the Indian turnip a member of the arum family, the tiger tail a member of the lily family. For many of the herbs there are three or more different names. A botanist may call one vine *Rhus radicans* but to the swampers it was cow itch, and the rest of us know it as poison ivy.

On one score there is no argument whatever. The profusion of plant

The placid-looking plants at right are insect eaters. In the Okefenokee they grow in wet, acid soil that is poor in nitrogen and phosphates, main elements in the making of proteins. Lacking enough sustenance from the earth, the plants get it from the bodies of insects, which they trap and ingest.

The types of traps vary. Sundews and butterworts (near right) exude a sticky substance that turns them into a natural kind of flypaper. Pitcher plants (far right, top) have a tubular "pitcher" with a slick lining that prevents insects from climbing back out once in. Bladderworts (far right, bottom) ensnare their prey by means of a host of vesicles—tiny bladder-like vessels —growing from their leaves. Each vesicle is equipped with a trap-door device, and when an insect trips this mechanism the door slams shut.

FLY TRAPPED ON SUNDEW

YELLOW BUTTERWORT

TUBES OF A PITCHER PLANT

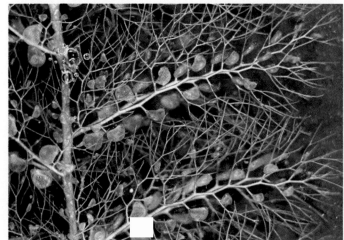

UNDERWATER LEAVES OF A BLADDERWORT

life in the Okefenokee and the long growing season produce as spectacular a floral display as can be seen anywhere in the South. In February, the bell-shaped white flowers of the highbush huckleberries first show, followed by the pink flowers of the hurrah bushes, the tiny white flowers of the climbing heath and the flaming blossoms of the red maple. In February, too, the flowers of the red chokeberries appear, presaging an early crop of berries. The chokeberry blossoms are followed by the almost explosive appearance of the neverwets thrusting up immeasurable numbers of their golden clubs. In March come the flowers of wampee and rose pogonia, wild azaleas and swamp iris, white water lily and old man's cologne.

The rush of flowers goes on into a maturing of summer blossoms, among them magnolia and miller's maid and cow lily. The many species of bladderwort ensure a continuity of flowers into the fall, putting up purple or yellow flowers on long, slender stems, or clusters of minuscule white blossoms crouched against the peat muck. These flowers endure through October, or even November.

The blooms are displayed at times guaranteed to get as much attention as possible from the pollinating butterflies, moths, flies and bees. In this perfect place for hunting nectar, the bees move from golden water lilies to cassena hollies, from purple water shields to the blue blossoms of pickerelweeds, and then to the flowers of huckleberries, gallberries, titis and palmettos. The honey they produce is distinctively flavored by the different blossoms of the seasons. The swampers esteemed the delicacy they found in the combs, but they had to fight to reach it ahead of the black bears.

The more I came to know the Okefenokee, the sharper grew my realization of how beautifully the swamp's "crops" of food interlock with the needs of its creatures. Different kinds of food serve the needs of multitudes of different lives, most visibly in the case of the almost continuous crops of different kinds of berries. Not only are the berries plentiful, often overwhelmingly so, but many of them linger on their stalks for months, providing a larder of food for mammal and bird alike. Wild turkeys loft to the tops of black-gum trees to strip them of their pea-sized berries. Black bears gorge on huckleberries, their muzzles running with dark juice, their droppings purple on the forest floor.

The huckleberry, blueberry, blackberry and gum berry are among the most common fruits, but there are many other, smaller crops. On almost every journey I made through the swamp I saw berries hiding in thickets, spattered over thousands of large bushes, revealing blues and greens and reds and purples and blacks. The green berries of the smilax, clustered on their vines, ripen when the first frosts hit the Okefenokee, perhaps as early as November or December. Cold weather is also the ripening agent for such berries as the swamp redbay and the cassena. This crop comes at a time when much other vegetation is dead or dying, and helps many of the berry eaters get through the winter, until the huckleberries begin ripening again.

The frost was yet to come when I finished my survey of the plants of the Okefenokee. The time was late October, and I found it hard to believe that winter would begin in about a month. The autumn winds were balmy, the skies clear, the sun hot enough to sunburn. Yet, despite the warmth, the swamp showed signs of moving into winter. The leaves of many of the shrubs were falling, sinking to shallow peat bottoms and suffusing the water with a red richness when the sun splashed on them. The suffusive greens of the cypresses were fading, turning amber, brown and gold. The flowers had mostly withdrawn. A few white lilies sat in lonely seclusion among sunning turtles and alligators. Solitary bladderworts thrust up lavender flowers while scattered flocks of ducks appeared, reconnoitering a bit before settling down to make a winter of it feeding on prairie plants.

Throughout the swamp, late autumn is a time of impatience for the human observer because so little seems to be happening. For the plants it is a time of rest, a preparation for their next skirmish in the grand design of filling in the swamp.

The Venerable Cypress

Few scenes evoke the mood of the swamp more swiftly than a stand of stately cypress trees, their ash-gray or reddish-brown trunks set on massive fluted bases and their branches bearded with gray Spanish moss. The most common tree in the Okefenokee, the pond cypress, occupies almost four fifths of the swamp. Another species, the American bald cypress, is also found there. Descendants of trees that covered a good part of North America about 70 million years ago, these two cypresses now thrive all across the southern coastal plain and along the Mississippi Valley as far north as Illinois.

The cypress, actually a member of the coniferous redwood family, is an unusual tree. Unlike such other conifers as pines, spruces and firs, the cypress is deciduous; it loses its needles in the fall. It readily takes to water, doing well even when its base is completely submerged. To achieve stability in such an environment, the tree has a swollen base from which heavy roots reach out horizontally in all directions, burying themselves in the sandy soil or peat at the bottom of the swamp. Thus buttressed, a cypress is seldom blown down, even during a windstorm.

Characteristic of the cypresses are the knees that grow from the lateral roots, either remaining submerged or poking up above the surface of the water. The function of these curious protuberances, which may be a few inches to several feet tall, is unknown. Some botanists believe that they help stabilize a tree since some of its roots grow from the knees. According to another theory, the knees help aerate the trees in their waterlogged habitat; but careful studies have failed to turn up any proof of this. Perhaps the explanation offered by another expert makes the most sense—the knees are simply useless growths, like warts.

Lumber companies have long coveted the Okefenokee's vast quantities of valuable cypress. Lumbering operations that began in 1909 took more than 400 million board feet of cypress out of the swamp. By 1927 the more profitable stands had all been cut over and the lumbermen stopped work. But despite this extensive logging there are still 400-year-old cypress giants growing in the swamp today, some of them 120 feet tall. With most of the Okefenokee now a federal refuge, it is likely that in centuries to come the successors to these trees will live to the same ripe old age.

An ancient bald cypress, half its crown blasted away by wind or sheared off by lightning, rises solidly on its buttressed trunk by the side of the Suwannee River. This veteran specimen, more than 70 feet tall, has weathered hurricane, fire and drought in the swamp for some 300 years.

Of the two kinds of cypresses that flourish together in Southern swamp areas, the bald cypress has characteristic "open" needles (above) that fan out from the smaller branches.

The pond cypress, more numerous than the bald cypress, has "closed" needles (below) lying flat along the branches, which usually grow more horizontally than on the bald cypress.

Bald cypresses (background) tower over their shorter relatives, the pond cypresses, as autumn begins to clothe both varieties with color.

The massive conical bases of two bald cypresses rise from swamp water that covers the heavy lateral roots anchoring the trees. Cypresses can stand firm even in 75- to 80-mile-per-hour gales. Their stability depends partly on their anchor roots and partly on the great weight of their bases, which may be three or four times bigger around than the rest of the trunk.

Rarely exposed in this fashion, great roots radiate from a pond cypress. Normally the roots are not seen, but a combination of factors has laid them bare: a drop in the water level followed by either a flood that washed away the muck covering the roots or a fire that burned off the surrounding peat. The tree may die because of the resulting lack of sustenance.

Knobby cypress knees protrude through the water from the submerged roots of a bald-cypress tree. These weird and strangely contorted forms, which are hollow and only thinly covered with bark, sometimes grow close to the tree's trunk but often pop up three or four feet away from it.

Like dignified old soldiers on dress parade, ranks of cypresses line the reflecting waters of Minnie's Lake in midsummer. The lake, in the

center of the Okefenokee, is actually a wide part of the Suwannee River, and is clear of the plants that clog other swamp waterways.

6/ The Track of the Bear

Then he saw the bear. It did not emerge, appear: it was just there, immobile, fixed in the green and windless noon's hot dappling, not as big as he had dreamed it but as big as he had expected, bigger. WILLIAM FAULKNER/ THE BEAR

The season is now late autumn. The air is warm and the sun still hot on odd days. Ducks pour in from the North, clots of scaup speeding across Chesser Prairie, mallard settling on Chase Prairie, green-winged teal feeding along the fringes of Grand Prairie. The warblers are filtering through the swamp. Some will stay for the winter; others will go south. Sudden influxes of southbound robins smother clearings and trees everywhere in the swamp.

With the year in the Okefenokee coming to a close, I am making a very special trip. From where I stand at the moment, at a point in the east-central part of the swamp, I cannot see any bird movements at all, because I am surrounded by a claustrophobic landscape: thickets of hurrah bush and black bamboo, looming cypresses blotting out patches of the sky. In the confinement of the landscape, my vision goes nowhere. I have to reassure myself that I am halfway to Bugaboo Island, that the Suwannee Canal is 3,000 feet behind me, that I have left my canoe there. My footprints have filled in; my passage has left no trace in the quagmire peat. A white ribbon hangs in a huckleberry bush at my back; with the other ribbons I have left as markings along the way, it will guide me back to the canal and my canoe. Looking ahead into the trees and the endless smilax gripping the endless bushes, I feel the presence of the swamp heavy all around me.

Bugaboo Island draws the traveler partly because, like the mountain, it is there. Tantalizingly close to the man-made water roads of the swamp—only about a mile from the Suwannee Canal—it is yet so difficult to reach as to be beyond any casual walk. I have tried to reach it once before, with an old swamper, Doc Ryder, to guide me, but the effort defeated even him. Floyd's Island, only about six miles to the north, and Billy's Island, about four miles to the west, are accessible with relative ease. But Bugaboo remains one of the most isolated of all the islands in the Okefenokee.

Another reason Bugaboo entices a man, and has done so since Josiah Mizell discovered the place in 1874, is that it has always been a paradise for game and other mammals of the swamp. Deer find good grazing in its environs; bobcats prowl there, and their prey—raccoons, rabbits, opossums, squirrels—abound; flourishing armies of small animals of the woods, such as cotton rats, shrews and moles, make their homes beneath the island's thick carpet of pine needles; in the shallow waters around it otters play and fish; and, of course, there is the black bear, lording it over all other creatures.

Altogether, there are 48 species of mammals in the Okefenokee, and most of them are represented on Bugaboo. In the main these animals, including several species of bats, are night creatures and therefore hard to see, but it seemed to me well worth the exertion of mushing out to Bugaboo to find out at least what their realm was like.

There were some things I had learned about Bugaboo in advance. I knew, for example, that at an earlier time some logging had been undertaken there, a minor operation compared to the booming enterprise at Billy's Island. I had been told, too, that the only trace of man not yet erased by swamp growth is the faint mark of a ditch cut out presumably to ease the transport of the logs away from the island. I am now trying to follow this shadowy trail, but I keep losing it.

I have, in fact, begun to question the wisdom of my decision to make the trip at all. Struggling in deep muck that abruptly becomes deeper, exhausted by each step forward, I am moving at a snail's pace—perhaps 30 feet per minute. I am learning why such boglands remain largely unseen by man; they are virtually impassable.

The animals that live in this part of the swamp seem to cope with such difficulties. I notice, for instance, that deer trails crisscross the bog here. The deer in the Okefenokee are the common whitetails found throughout Eastern America, but in the swamp they seem different, perhaps because the softness of the ground makes it impossible for them to make use of their fantastic ability to leap—anywhere from 10 to 20 feet in one bound. Also, they seem more timid in the Okefenokee. They are heard often enough as they browse in thickets, but they are seen only for a second, as with one flash of their uplifted tails they disappear into distant trees.

But to tell the truth, I am not thinking much about deer as I slog along. Mostly I am thinking about bears. Even if they are no longer abundant in the swamp—there are reputed to be only around 150—they are still very much a presence, and they leave many trails as they move across the boglands. Now in November there are signs of bears everywhere along the eastern side of the swamp: claw marks on a black gum on Cowhouse Island, saplings scarred and ripped on Floyd's Island, broken branches at the end of the main reach of the Suwannee Canal.

The ripped and clawed trees are territorial signs recognized by other bears. Apparently a bear that wants to establish its claim to a territory will stretch up to its full height and scratch its claw marks on a tree. The next bear to come along may test its reach against the other's; failing that test, it keeps on moving, but if its scratch marks are higher, the newcomer can then stake a claim to that territory. When the first bear returns and sees that it has been bested, it must find another turf. A civilized way of managing a potentially violent situation.

These black bears of the Okefenokee, the only kind there, are the same species—*Ursus americanus*—as those in the Rockies and farther west. But in the East they are almost always black while in the West they may be black, brown or cinnamon colored. They are the smallest of North American bears—and the most common, though they have been forced by men to retreat ever deeper into the wilderness.

Unlike the bears at Yellowstone National Park, which can be seen standing around waiting for handouts, the bears of the Okefenokee are extremely wary. This is a good thing not only for the bears but also for any humans who might meet up with one. An adult bear can weigh almost 500 pounds and measure anywhere from four to five feet from tail to snout. When it stands erect to attack, its forepaws and claws outstretched, its next move unpredictable, it is danger incarnate. Such encounters in the swamp are increasingly rare, however. The bears know where men are and avoid them—although they also know the islands where canoeists stop, and regularly pillage the garbage of the campers at night. Basically, a black bear is a loner even with its own kind, and tends to be quarrelsome except for a short and intensely affectionate courting period in the summer. During the hot weather, when not courting, the bears slump in damp places to cool off. Old swampers claim that bears sometimes bite chunks out of pine trees on the swamp islands, let the trees bleed for half a day, then roll themselves against the trunks so that the pitch smothers their black hides. Then, with the glutinous stuff stuck all over them, they roll in sand or earth or leaves. This odd behavior (which has not been confirmed by naturalists) might be a protection against the biting flies that infest the swamp in summer. Uncle Will Cox said that a gum-smeared bear is a blood-curdling sight— "like meetin' some kind of a monster out there."

As the days get colder the bears prepare for winter by becoming fat and sleepy. They are not, however, true hibernators; they rouse themselves intermittently during this semidormant period and, indeed, the females give birth at this time. They are very protective of their cubs, especially in the vicinity of alligators, which find a cub a juicy morsel. Reciprocally, bears fancy young alligators, and any female gator unwise enough to try to defend her young from a full-grown bear is unlikely to forget the experience. In the old days cattle were also the target of bears; I was told that a bear of even medium size could break the neck of an ox with one blow. Normally, though, a bear hunts small prey by digging into burrows, smashing rotten logs, overturning rocks. Usually, it keeps silent while hunting, except for occasional grunts; in the case of larger prey, it stalks with a silence so complete it is astonishing, then makes a lightning charge with those powerful forepaws.

I had seen a fresh bear pawprint once on Billy's Island, water still seeping into it; the impression of five toes and a sole about seven inches long gave it the look almost of a human footprint. And I learned firsthand about the bear's remarkable stealth just a few days before this venture to Bugaboo, as I was paddling along the main water trail between Big Water and Minnie's Lake. From my canoe I heard a great crashing in a nearby cypress bay, the sound of a juggernaut moving. I sat still, listening, sensing that the sound was approaching. It did indeed come closer. Then, as abruptly as if cut by a knife, the sound stopped, so close that I momentarily expected the bear to step out of the bushes to confront me. But there was only silence. Later I asked Jewett Hall, who was born on Billy's Island and now works for the federal refuge, how a bear could approach so closely and then disappear without a sound. "When a bear thinks he's alone, he don't much care how much noise he makes," Hall said. "But when he smells an enemy, he's as silent as a snake." I knew Hall was right, but I still did not understand how that bear could have moved so quietly through thickets of huckleberries and smilax when the ground was littered with dried leaves, branches and twigs. I had found the bear's path, a ragged track smashed through bushes. It would be a roadway, Hall told me, for deer and other animals to use later.

Now, on my way to Bugaboo, I come across another such rough trail, broken across the surface of the bog. I assume that if it is the track of a bear, the beast is either going to or coming from the island, and I feel bound to follow its path. Still, as I do so, lurching, slipping, rising only to slip again, the possibility of the bear's presence adds a distinctly disquieting new element to my journey. With one leg or the other buried in muck I am a long way from the securities of civilization, and certainly potentially easy prey. I wonder again whether my venture is illuminating or merely foolhardy.

Perversely, since it is scarcely calculated to comfort a man slogging alone through a bog, I keep thinking of some of the fearsome tales of bears in the swamp, and of one in particular, reported by A. S. McQueen and Hamp Mizell in their *History of Okefenokee Swamp.* The authors tell of a bear called Old Soker who in the 1880s killed and maimed many bear dogs. The swampers who studied its huge prints believed it to be at least as big as a grizzly. *Ursus horribilis,* the Latin name for the grizzly, is an apt one; in the wild this terror can weigh up to 800 pounds and measure seven feet long.

Old Soker's predations were infamous even at a time when the swamp people were all too aware of bears' insatiable appetite for hogs, cows, dogs and chickens. To keep any kind of domestic animals the swampers had to enclose them in miniature fortresses made of logs; even the chickens were locked inside wooden stockades.

One morning, infuriated by a particularly audacious hog raid by Old Soker, Dave Mizell and his son Harley set forth, shotguns in hand. They left their dogs behind; any yapping would have destroyed their hope of surprising the bear. They tracked it for hours. The trail was deeply imprinted in the muck, and it was clear that they were following a monster. They crossed Chesser Prairie, flanked Chase Prairie, and finally reached the area where I am now laboriously trying to walk. Dave Mizell circled an island, probably Bugaboo, while his son set out to investigate the interior.

The younger Mizell found the bear track zigzagging across the island through thick bushes and followed it. Perhaps Old Soker had grown contemptuous of men without dogs, for when Harley came out of a

A watchful opossum perches in a black-gum tree, its long tail wrapped around the trunk for support. A nocturnal creature, the opossum is related to the kangaroo and other marsupials. Its young, born not fully developed after a 13-day gestation period, spend two months completing their initial growth in a pouch on the mother's belly.

thicket and stood up to look around, he found himself face to face with his quarry. Like all swampers, Harley was a quick shot; he fired at close range and hit the bear in the shoulder. Old Soker fell, bounded up, and disappeared into the bushes. Dave Mizell, having heard the shot, waited for the animal to break cover. When it burst out of the island's trees, he brought it down with a full shotgun charge. Old Soker was 11 feet from "tip to tip." If the Mizells measured accurately, its body alone was more than seven feet long. The swampers had been right. Old Soker was as big as a grizzly.

The track of the bear I am following leads into a thicket that overhangs a run of dark water. It would be easier to slip into the water than to smash through the thicket, but the possibility that I may stumble upon a submerged alligator gives me pause. I choose instead to force my way through the thicket. The maze of shrubs is so dense that I almost miss seeing several apparently lifeless brown shapes dangling in the branches. They are Seminole bats, hanging upside down in day sleep.

Thousands of bats live in the swamp, three species in particular—the Seminole, the pipistrelle and the evening bat. They appear at dusk along watercourses everywhere, more felt than seen, silently punctuating the night life of the swamp as they whisk by. The pipistrelles are the most elusive of the three species, the smallest bats in the United States —weighing between one sixth and one quarter of an ounce. Curiously, they are relatively poor fliers, and must rest frequently in their night flights in search of food. Now, in the fall, they would have reached their maximum weight in readiness for hibernation.

The Seminoles are the most visible bats, deep mahogany in color with a slight frosting of white hairs. I have seen them in many places in the swamp, spiraling down on narrow wings from high flight in the dusky air. They are quite unlike the pipistrelles, being twice the weight —if a top weight of half an ounce can be imagined as relatively gigantic. Unlike most of the swamp bats, which hibernate in the winter—the only mammals in the swamp that truly hibernate—the Seminoles migrate south instead.

Occasionally, here and there in the Okefenokee, I have spotted evening bats, easy to identify because they are such slow and deliberate fliers and because they favor tree hollows for sleeping. I have sometimes come upon them there while looking for insects, birds' nests and snakes. The bats hunt throughout the swamp, and their echo-location guidance system—ultrasonic cries bouncing back from obstructions—seems to work just as well for them in trees festooned with Spanish moss as it does in thick shrubbery.

The Seminole bats I have just disturbed by my blundering flutter off to resume their sleep elsewhere. I am glad to have seen them in the sunlight, out of their element, as it were. It somehow puts me more in touch with the secret inner life of the swamp that many visitors never see. I have missed much of this life on previous journeys in the Okefenokee. Small swamp mammals, their comings and goings unobtrusive, seldom show themselves. The eastern mole burrows through the sand of nearly all the islands, eating about half its own weight in insects and vegetation every day. Even less visible is the round-tailed muskrat, also known as the Florida water rat, a secretive, half-pound rodent that lives in the swamps in thousands. This creature makes a globular nest of dried grasses about two feet in diameter and builds it on the sphagnum moss at water level so that the entrance to the nest is concealed. If escape is necessary, the occupant of the nest flees through exits dug down into the sphagnous muck and thence into watery tunnels.

Suddenly, almost from under my feet, a small, rust-colored creature with coarse fur and short ears bursts into motion and bounds lightly across the bogland. The marsh rabbit, one of the many species of cottontail, never ceases to fascinate me as an example of the power of unlikely creatures to fit into strange environments. Somehow, this rabbit —which is fond of coastal islands, heavily vegetated swamps and bottomlands—has found it advantageous to occupy a watery world teeming with enemies; despite the alligators, it does not hesitate to dive into deep water, particularly along the Suwannee River, and swim strongly for the farther shore. It is smaller than both the ubiquitous eastern cottontail and the marsh rabbit of Louisiana, Mississippi and Texas.

Even more strange in its adaptation to the Okefenokee environment is the armadillo. When I first saw one of these small armored mammals scuttling along a trail near Stephen Foster State Park in the western side of the swamp, I was nonplussed because nothing I knew about the animal connected it in my mind with swamps. What was the armadillo, which thrives in dry, hot areas of the Southwest and Mexico, doing here? Apparently this burrowing creature was introduced into Florida some years ago; then it extended its range north into the swamp, where it was first seen in 1963. It seems to manage very well in the Okefenokee, perhaps because its classic enemy, the coyote, has never infiltrated the swamp. Despite the armored shell—the armadillo looks like a tank the size of a house cat—it somehow draws enough air into

A white-tailed doe and her fawns, in characteristic summer coats, eye the photographer who has interrupted their browse on Chesser Island. Fawns shed their spots within their first year, and thereafter take on the plain coloring of the adults—blue-gray in winter and reddish in summer. The species gets its name from patches of white on the underside of the tail, clearly visible when raised in flight.

its lungs so that it can actually swim. Even without air to make it buoyant, it can walk underwater for short distances.

The armadillo embodies the triumph of all those dry-land creatures that roam freely through a world that looks as though it should belong solely to the water animals. Before my first visit to the swamp, I had thought it must be dominated by the alligator. Actually, the bear has always been king of the Okefenokee. But at one time another land mammal challenged even the bear—the wild boar. Between 30 and 50 years ago the piney woods rooter, as it was called, was perhaps the most pervasive and truly dangerous animal in the swamp, capable not only of killing bears in titanic fights, but of taking on and dispatching diamondback rattlesnakes. No one is quite sure where the piney woods rooters came from, only that they were finally hunted out. They may have been survivors of swine brought to America by de Soto and other Spaniards in the early 16th Century. The swampers never hunted them unless they were well armed and accompanied by trained dogs that could put these formidable beasts to flight or bring them to bay for shooting. The rooters invariably turned to fight at the end and the hunter always risked his dogs.

In time the rooters interbred with razorback hogs, escapees from the pens of the swampers. Many of them were done in because of their special fondness for the bulbous root of the wampee plant, a root so hot it can burn a person's throat. Wampee fattened them like no other food. Greedy for it, they became careless of their enemies. The bears found them at dusk on land and in the shallow prairie waters. They proved easy victims; they stood so long in the shallows digging for the roots that the water eventually softened their hooves, and they could hardly walk, let alone run.

The track I am following has disappeared; apparently the bear has made a turn inside a thicket. By this time, half exhausted, I am all the more appreciative of the toughness of the two Mizells, who must have circled a score of thickets in their pursuit of Old Soker.

I calculate that I have traveled more than two thirds of the way to Bugaboo by now, and I yearn for the appearance of its tall pines ahead. But the exertion, the oppressive atmosphere and the fear of being lost do not encourage clear thinking or hearing. A scream sounds from somewhere. Is it the cry of a catbird close at hand—or of some larger creature a distance away? I remember Uncle Will Cox saying that the cry of a cougar sounded like "a woman hollerin'." He was convinced that cougars still prowled the swamp. They came into it periodically, he said, from coastal wilderness areas, and he insisted he had seen one on Cowhouse Island in "nineteen and fifty-four."

He may be right. The last officially recognized sighting of a cougar occurred in 1958, and a swamp brochure notes that the big brown cat may still enter the Okefenokee occasionally. From my position now, up to the knees in muck, it is difficult to imagine a world less suited to a big cat, and yet the cougar is known to have ranged widely throughout the swamp in former years. Uncle Will had told me of reliable signs of the cat I could watch for on my way to Bugaboo—deep claw marks in logs and tree trunks, scratch marks in the earth where the cougar buried its excrement or the covered carcass of a half-eaten victim. The cougar's body can measure more than seven feet; it weighs about 250 pounds and is capable of killing much heavier animals. Reviewing these facts as I struggle in the muck, I find no comfort in Uncle Will's cheerful conviction about the cougar's survival.

The cry comes again. This time I recognize it: a bobcat. They are everywhere in the swamp, though hardly ever seen. I surprised one on Billy's Island in broad daylight in late spring, and saw another on Pine Island very early another morning, its yard-long brown body flowing headfirst down the trunk of a tree before bounding away on springsteel legs. The bobcat, like the bear and the raccoon, hunts all through the swamp: the cypress bays, the sphagnous bogs, the pine barrens, the hammocks, the canal banks. Even in times past when the swamp teemed with hunting dogs, with armed men, with loggers and trappers, the bobcat was difficult prey. It could outrun any dog; it could zigzag, run back on its tracks, climb trees and jump into bogs to break the scent path. It could catch and kill fawns just as easily as it hunted rabbits and cotton rats, young hogs and sheep, and wild turkeys.

Much smaller than the cougar (adult males seldom reach 40 pounds), the bobcat swims very well for a cat. Its short tail—averaging about five inches—has given it its name. Unlike the cougar, which usually runs a straight path, the inquisitive bobcat pursues a crooked trail as it detours to investigate objects that arouse its interest. It is a night traveler by nature and stalks small mammals with its eyes and nose, though if it misses a kill it is apt to give up the chase. It has many cries, several of them sounding like the yowls of domestic cats, and it sometimes plays with its smaller catches the way house cats do with mice.

The swampers hated and feared both bear and cougar, but mixed with the hate and fear was some respect for the power of these animals. The bobcat enjoyed no such esteem. When the men found one in their traps they spent a happy half-hour beating the trapped animal with sticks until it was exhausted or its mangled legs gave out. The brutality could be mindless. Jackson Lee described how swampers would shoot a treed bobcat with bird shot, aiming for its hindquarters to cripple it. The bobcat would jump for freedom, and "then you'd see some fun with the dogs," Lee said. In half a century about 1,000 bobcats were slain in the Okefenokee. And yet the bobcat survived. It became secretive, more seldom seen, a fugitive in the forest, and it held its own. Now protected, it breeds well and maintains a stable population estimated at about 700.

With the general decline in the population of larger predators, some parts of the swamp have been taken over by the raccoon. For many years it was kept in its proper place in the Okefenokee, a skulking night-hunter that lived at the mercy of the big carnivores. As these diminished in number, the raccoon population soared.

On my journeys through the swamp I have seen more raccoons than I could possibly count. I have seen them stuffing themselves with huckleberries, reaching for dahoon berries in lofty trees and moving along the banks of the canal at dusk looking for frogs, small turtles and turtle eggs. The raccoon also loves crayfish, and its passion for these swamp-bottom creatures is such that it will dig for them in deep mud even though the nearby waters move with the surge and splash of alligators. In fact, this greedy little predator even covets the eggs of that fearsome neighbor. Once I came across a raccoon frantically digging for eggs in an alligator nest, so intent on its work that it did not even look up when I shone a flashlight on it.

Nothing is safe from the Okefenokee's raccoons. It is almost impossible to camp anywhere in the swamp without being burglarized by them. One night my pack was unstrapped, its contents scattered for yards, and every available scrap of food removed. The thieves even came into my tent and tugged at my sleeping bag.

Much less visible in the Okefenokee are the otters, which share a rather uneasy occupation of the swamp's waters with the alligators. Like the raccoons, otters stick to the cypress bays during the summer and strike out on wider-ranging expeditions only in the colder weather when the alligators become torpid. This graceful, beautiful creature is the finest fisherman in the swamp, and its playful habits and its mastery of both land and water engaged the imaginations of the old swamp

Still thriving in the Okefenokee, the bobcat strongly resembles the ordinary house cat but is actually a species of Canadian lynx, with the short tail and mottled fur that are characteristic of the lynx family. A fierce fighter, the bobcat prowls by night for small mammals and birds, and often beds down by day in hollow logs.

settlers. Because there are no high banks in the swamp, the otters cannot play their favorite game of sliding down mudbanks, but they do kick themselves across the boglands, skidding on their bellies. They communicate with a *kuk-kuk-kuk* noise and high-pitched chirps that sounded to the swampers like the cries of cardinals.

But engaging as the otters were, the value of their fur was more attractive still. In the 1920s their glossy brown pelt had a $20 price tag. Otters are gregarious fellows, fond of companionable gatherings, and they used common tracks through the swamp so that men found them easy to catch. The swampers placed toothed traps on the tracks; or they chopped hollows in the tops of logs where the otters rested, put traps inside and covered the traps with trash. One youngster trained a dog to chase otters into underwater refuge holes, and would kill the creatures there by driving down sharp-pointed sticks.

So for a while the otter was headed for extinction. But the creation of the wildlife refuge in 1937 put a stop to the trappers' depredations and the otter began a slow recovery. Now several hundred of them inhabit the swamp. But they keep more to themselves than the ubiquitous raccoon, and I never saw one, though I once followed the underwater trace of one otter 100 yards or so, its spoor a trail of muddy debris kicked up by its webbed feet. Maybe on my next trip to the Okefenokee I will have the pleasure of meeting an otter in the flesh.

The pines of Bugaboo Island finally loom up just ahead of me. It has taken me more than three hours to travel the mile from the Suwannee Canal. I struggle through the last of the muck and lie down gratefully on the pine-needled ground. At the foot of the pines, low-growing palmettos thrive in the sandy soil. I know that the island has its share of rattlesnakes, and I keep a wary eye open for them. As I look around, I realize that Bugaboo is not much different from any other island in the Okefenokee. But because it is so difficult to get to, it has preserved its state of isolation from man, its role as an ultimate refuge. Lying there in a silence that is complete except for the faint cry of a red-shouldered hawk, I experience a sense of utter solitude that is in its way as satisfying as the fulfillment I feel at having achieved my goal.

But nothing is ever really still for very long in the swamp. A stirring in the pines high above draws my eye to a gray squirrel whisking along a branch. The gray squirrel—cat squirrel, the swampers called it—was so common that Jackson Lee and two of his sons shot 26 of them in one day's hunting in the 1920s. Then, because the peregrine falcons, ospreys, hawks and eagles were shot out too, the barred owl increased its numbers. The barred owl loved squirrels. So another world was created in which it was tougher for the gray squirrel to survive. But the men had come and gone, and nature had restored some kind of balance. The gray squirrel, one of the fastest-breeding mammals, is again common in the forests of the swamp.

It is easy to rest on Bugaboo and ruminate, less easy to contemplate my return journey to the canal. I know I must leave the island in time to reach the canal before dark. Reluctantly, I get up. I haven't time, or in fact the energy, to walk its two-mile length. Neither can I follow the faint line of the filled-in logging ditch that I know must touch the island somewhere on its other side. I must instead follow my trail of ribbons back to the canal. As I start to walk, dreading the prospect, a large figure dressed in black abruptly stands up in some nearby bushes. For a second, I think it is a man. A five-foot man in a shaggy black coat, ears short and rounded, furry face coming to a brown point at the nose. The bear looks at me, those lethal paws extended. I hold my breath; I have no idea what the beast's next move will be—then it utters a loud, whining cry, almost human, turns and crashes away.

For another second, as I stand there frozen, I could be one of the Mizells, my shotgun smoking in my hand, the great black figure toppling. I think of vengeful swampers beating bobcats to death, of hunting parties of lumbermen, of packs of hunting dogs, of cougars, boars and alligators. I plunge back into the clinging muck of the swamp, not exactly scared, but very much looking forward to the Suwannee Canal, and the familiar feel of my canoe.

NATURE WALK / In the Autumnal Swamp

PHOTOGRAPHS BY ROBERT WALCH

Superficially all journeys in the Okefenokee may seem repetitive: a series of winding watercourses among meadows of jostling plants, colonnades of statuesque trees, claustrophobic thickets of shrubs and vines. But in fact every Okefenokee trip is unique because the swamp is a synthesis of countless changes occurring every second. To the newcomer these alterations are not noticeable except with the seasons, which do change even in this Southern swamp. But then the eye becomes more educated. Variations can be seen day to day, then minute to minute, moment to moment. In the fall especially, the swamp becomes a giant kaleidoscope of change, with decay and death preparing the way for the exuberant regeneration to come in the months that follow.

Well before sunrise one morning in the late fall we entered the Okefenokee from Camp Cornelia at the eastern end of the Suwannee Canal; our destination was Gannet Lake, about ten and a half miles down a wandering watercourse. In the predawn gloom the canoe skimmed along the dusky, marble-smooth canal into dense mist. On either side were hints of the transformation that the swamp continually undergoes. A broken shrub bough hung down into the water, catching a small arc of leaves in the languid current, along with a dead bittern, twigs, algae, some chunks of uprooted peat. Tomorrow these prisoners of the current might be massed more thickly, or be gone altogether.

After paddling about two miles, we turned south from the canal and slid into the broad grassy swamplands known as Chesser Prairie. Now the air lightened and the mist glowed, became luminous and alive; the prairie became visible in the early brightness of dawn. Bur marigolds bloomed in yellow clusters. Presently the strengthening sun would drive the mist from the leaf-spattered water, then chase it among the distant cypresses where it usually clings until an hour or so before noon.

Almost all the prairies of the swamp look as if they had been landscaped by man. Their arrangement of floating water plants in the foreground, patches of upright spires and clumps of various grasses in the middle ground, with odd clumps of shrubs and trees here and there, all lead the eye away to a horizon beautifully dignified with stately lines of cypresses. The cypresses, their fibrous bark splotched with gray-green lichen, remind me of man-sculptured vistas: the garden-lined pools behind Versailles Palace, the intricate hedgerow maze at Hampton Court, the precisely planted rows of chestnut trees along the Champs Elysées. But the Okefenokee prairies, architectured in wild form and reaching out of sight, also present in-

FOLIOSE LICHEN ON A CYPRESS

numerable landscapes beyond the artistic capability of man.

Now, with the glow of the hidden sun expanding, Chesser Prairie appeared to be a painted landscape, permanent, unchanging, motionless. Yet I knew it was nothing of the sort. Every plant before us—from the scaly lichens coating a young cypress trunk to the clots of dead grass adrift in the sluggish water—was part of the never-ending struggle to transform the swamp. These plants

BUR MARIGOLDS IN CHESSER PRAIRIE

SPANISH MOSS OVERHANGING A CYPRESS KNEE

pack the prairie from one end to the other with such a density of growth that in time, barring fires, it could be transformed into ground that would sprout cypress, pine and bay trees.

From the middle of the prairie, with the sun appearing as a hazy, glaring disk through the eastern cypresses, this process was not clearly visible, particularly since most of the plants were either quiescent or had disappeared for the oncoming winter. It was not merely the plants that were quiescent now. Water that had previously swarmed with pig and cricket frogs, that had swirled with the passage of countless alligators, was unruffled. These creatures, although still visible from time to time, were preparing for winter dormancy; in a few months they would be hidden in trash on the bottom or buried in peaty muck. The fish that in spring and early summer had made the water sparkle with their activity were almost invisible, appearing only as occasional darts of silvery movement flashing among the scattered lily pads.

Floating Islands

But even in this period of repose the prairie was still active. Leaves and twigs rained down from the trees and shrubs, decomposing even before hitting the peat bottom. This decomposing detritus generates gas that, in turn, lifts masses of peat. Local people call these blow-ups or, less imaginatively, batteries. Some were chunks mere inches across; others were floating platforms as much as 100 feet long. Much of the gas-borne peat rises one hour and sinks the next as the gas holding it up leaks away. But wherever a battery endures, plants grow on it and finally transform it into a small forested island known as a house.

It was when we paddled over to the edge of the prairie, to where the heavy growth begins, that we really felt the presence of the plants. There the cypresses held complete sway. Their woody knees jutted up from the submerged roots like diseased excrescences. From many cypress branches great swatches of Spanish moss—a misnamed relative of pineapples—hung in thick gray curtains.

A few paddle strokes away maiden cane and spike rush covered the water with a blanket of dead and decaying vegetable matter. Floating nearby were masses of leaves shed by black-gum trees. Lining the banks

AN OSPREY NEST

were various types of evergreens, including hurrah bushes and the holly known as the cassena, a shrub that frequently grows as tall as a small tree. Countless red berries spoke of new generations of plants to come— plants that would make their own

assaults on the space and form of the prairie. Behind us, isolated in the middle of the prairie, was a monument to failure: a stark, dead cypress tree—overcome, perhaps, by the last big fire in the swamp. But it provided refuge for the solitary nest of an osprey, a rare bird in these parts in autumn. Overhead flights of herons, egrets and ibises winged into the swamp to begin the day's hunting.

Animated by birds, the autumnal prairies seemed to have life, but in their seasonal way they were dying. The water-lily leaves spread wide and green to the pale sun, but soon they would die and sink. The prairie grasses, a vivid green only two or three weeks ago, had turned gray-brown. Thousands of desiccated seed heads—the autumnal leftovers of yellow-eyed grass—stood camou-

SPIKE RUSH, UNDERWATER

RED FRUIT OF A MOSS-DRAPED CASSENA HOLLY

A FRAGRANT WATER LILY

WATER-LILY LEAVES

flaged against the drab background of the grasses. In this landscape of neutral colors and quiet decay, the odd flowers of floating hearts and other water lilies appeared as summer's last bright fling.

As we drifted on through the quiet prairie country, the bow of our canoe cut through a cluster of water lilies, upsetting the green leaves and exposing their wine-colored undersides. Along the edge of a well-established house of cypresses and other woody growth, we saw a scattering of hooded pitcher plants, their hollow, insect-trapping leaves slowly dying in a way that ensures the species' continued survival.

In death and in life this carnivorous plant shares a curious interdependence with a particular insect that it does not digest, the flesh fly. Each summer the female fly lays an egg inside the tubular, hair-studded leaf; the egg hatches into a large white maggot that thrives on moths

and other insects that blunder down into the digestive fluid that the plant secretes at the base of the leaf.

Then in the fall some instinct prompts the maggot to chew a circular groove in the plant tissue high

HOODED PITCHER PLANTS

on the leaf. This causes the hooded top to wither and slump over, closing the entrance to the leaf. Inside this safe shelter the maggot hibernates until early spring.

With the return of warm weather, the plant's hardy roots send up new and rapid growth. At this point the plant's hibernating visitor emerges from last year's dead leaves and completes its metamorphosis into a winged adult. In this form the flesh fly apparently pays its debt to the host plant by pollinating its early-blooming flower, thus guaranteeing a vital supply of pitcher-plant seeds.

By such devices life persists everywhere amid signs of death—this I knew. Yet it was hard for me to imagine the fever of life-giving activity among the plants that had created the prairie landscape before us. The first plants to establish themselves on the batteries, getting a grip on the chunks of peat floating up from the bottom, had been the ubiq-

YELLOW-EYED GRASS AND LILY PADS IN GRAND PRAIRIE

uitous maiden canes and redroots, broom sedges and spike rushes, arrowheads and beak rushes. These plants had entrenched themselves in many ways, some by sending down small parts of their stems that root in the muck, others by sending forth floating or wind-driven seeds. As the plants thickened their root systems, they accumulated a thick mat of material—part peat, part living plant tissue—spongy and yielding, yet just firm enough for a man to walk on.

As we passed one battery, I decided to test its firmness and stepped out of the canoe. But it proved to be a relatively new formation, only about six months old, and not yet solidly established. With a gurgling sound, my feet sank two or three inches into the compacted peat.

It looked like nothing more than black mud from which a few low grasses sprouted, but I knew that if I returned about six years hence this same battery would be hosting a whole new set of more ambitious plant migrants: the buttonbush and titi, the swamp fetterbush, and red and black bamboo vines. All of these woody plants would crowd together so thickly that they would eventually displace many of the original plant settlers.

Living Houses

As we paddled beyond Chesser Prairie and entered Grand Prairie, we passed batteries in every stage of development. After the second growth come more solid shrubs: the omnipresent hurrah bush, the sweet spire, the poor-man's-soap, whose crushed leaves yield a sap that can be worked into suds. An occasional cypress seedling would also take up residence. All these migrants ensure that the battery will eventually achieve a permanent bond with the peaty muck beneath.

After about 20 years, trees take over the battery and turn it into a full-fledged house. Often the pond cypresses are the first to appear,

BERRIES ON A BLACK BAMBOO VINE

their soft green foliage callow and vulnerable looking. Or perhaps a mixture of bay trees: white, red and loblolly will be in the vanguard. By this time, the house is secure enough to begin its next significant stage of development. But at any time during the October-to-April dry season, fire may destroy the growth, and then the whole peat-accumulating, house-building process will have to begin all over again.

We pushed the canoe through clinging masses of vegetation toward a nearby mature house. There cypresses of every size formed an almost unbroken phalanx, with odd pines scattered among them; the house stood solidly fixed. Beneath the towering cypresses the under-brush was choked with red-berried

A "HOUSE" OF CYPRESS AND PINE, FRINGED BY MAIDEN-CANE GRASS

Smilax laurifolia, a bamboo vine that is popularly called black bamboo even though the true bamboo is a species of grass rather than a vine. Here and there amid patches of green I saw flashes of yellow—the long necklaces of seed pods adorning the titi. This tough shrub, which ranges as far north as coastal Virginia, usually sheds its leaves every year in the cooler climates; but in the warm Okefenokee region it keeps some of its leaves all year round. At ground level were the inevitable beds of sphagnum moss and thickets of chain ferns. Redroots and maiden canes, the pioneer plants of the peat, appeared here in another pioneering role, now surrounding and extending the circumference of the tree island.

SEED PODS OF A TITI SHRUB

A BED OF SPHAGNUM MOSS

By the time we reached the middle of Grand Prairie, the day had become hot and clear. Occasionally we could glimpse water birds typical of these prairies—great blue herons, wood ducks, common egrets, sandhill cranes, anhingas, white ibises and wood ibises. But the prairie remained a world of plants. The struggle of the plants is no wonder to the botanist; he observes what is obvious—that plants will take hold where they can. But to the layman it is a small miracle that the force of millions of apparently insignificant lives can mold their world to their needs and eventually, if they are lucky, dominate it entirely.

Grand Prairie gives way eventually to an almost impenetrable thicket of shrubs that, over hundreds of years, have accumulated organic material under their roots until they appear to be living on solid land. On

RED AND GRAY LICHEN

sunny days at this time of year alligators bask here. Cassena hollies flourish, their silvery bark decorated with splashes of beautiful red crustose lichen. Through this thicket our

trail led tortuously until eventually we emerged into Gannet Lake.

Here a silent black expanse of water glowed in the late sun, punctuated by the slow movement of a large alligator. This was once a haunt of the graceful wood ibis, whose black-tipped wings led the swamp people to think they were seeing gannets—which also have black-tipped wings, but which are sea birds.

The lake was once undoubtedly as shallow as any prairie, and as choked with water plants. But a century ago a great fire so thoroughly burned a large pocket in the peat that plants that might otherwise have encroached upon it were somewhat inhibited. Instead, they grow around the edge of the lake—masses of titi and other shrubs, sedges, ferns and maiden canes. In time, if no catastrophe intervenes, they will overwhelm Gannet Lake.

But for now the lake remains open. The alligator climbed lazily out of the water and watched us curiously down its long, blunt, corrugated muzzle. We were as far south as you can paddle anywhere in the swamp; not many travelers go there, and the hour was getting late. But we delayed a few more minutes as the sun sank into the more open country to the west where Black Jack Island lay beyond the reach of either our boat or our legs, a wilderness beyond the grasp of man. The sun sank lower, a pallid disk in a silent sky. Ibises passed overhead on their way to roosting places on Chesser Prairie behind us, and we turned back reluctantly to follow them.

AN ALLIGATOR TAKING THE SUN

THE GANNET LAKE SHORELINE, OVERGROWN WITH TITI

7/ Ruin and Renewal by Fire

*A peat fire destroys every living thing that can't get
out of its way. The roots of a giant cypress
are burned away as readily as those of a hurrah bush.*

ROY MOORE, OKEFENOKEE REFUGE MANAGER/ *FIELD REPORT OF FIRE, 1955*

In winter, journeys through the swamp are endless driftings through
shallow, mahogany-dark water, mirror reflections all around, the light
smoking and writhing in the early mist. In my subjective vision they in-
voked a movie called *Last Year at Marienbad,* which eerily transported
the viewer along an ambiguous route that appeared to go somewhere
and yet ended up nowhere. A feeling of lurking disaster, touched with
an odd exhilaration, ran through the movie. So it was with the swamp
this winter. Though thousands of birds remained in the Okefenokee,
their voices were muted, instruments more of communication and warning than of the full-throated singing of the spring and summer breeding
seasons. Trees passed in funereal procession, the same trees I had seen
many times before, but now gaunt. No wind stirred the drooping gray
moss on the naked cypresses. Just as tamaracks do in northern bogs,
the cypresses had shed their foliage and dropped many of their twigs.
They are among the few species of conifers that lose their leaves with
the onset of cold, and the loss is the dominant and distinctive mark of
winter in the swamp, creating a series of austere, brooding landscapes.

Somber tones were now the leitmotiv everywhere I went in the Okefenokee. The grasses had turned brown or sere yellow; the flowers had
mostly gone; in the once-swelling green meadows of the prairies, the
plants were discolored and limp. The woody shrubs, though most of
them keep their leaves, were mainly clad in dull tans and grays and

faded greens; even those that retained splashes of dark red leaves seemed to have lost their vitality.

The drabness was accentuated by the dryness. Winter is the season of drought in the Okefenokee, sometimes only moderate if the rains have been steady and abundant enough to sustain water levels, sometimes severe, with the accompanying peril of fire. The autumn rains this year had been meager and the winter swamp I traveled looked as near to tinder-dry as a swamp can look. Perhaps that explained the sense of lurking disaster that seemed to pervade it. I recalled the husky, old-man voice of Uncle Will Cox prophesying: "Oh, she's gonna burn, all right, she's gonna burn good."

It began to occur to me that in my journeys through the swamp earlier in the year I had seen signs of dryness, but that as an outsider I had been unable to add them up. I remembered the brisk winds of March evaporating quantities of water. In April I had seen the water level visibly low on the trunks of young cypresses. On Billy's Island in early May I had come across a small pond, its water almost gone, from which the usual oak toads had disappeared; only a few cricket frogs were left. In the mudflats of other drying ponds I had lifted the edges of thick mats of grass and uncovered salamanders and water snakes hiding below, apparently waiting for rain to rescue them. I had traced the drag marks of alligators that had deserted shrinking pools and migrated to ponds deeper in the swamp. In places the earth had been cracking dry, in odd contrast to the swampland just a few feet away.

In short, I had been an unwitting observer of potential crisis in the swamp, and the rains of summer had only served to keep me unaware. More than once, on a steaming August day, I had been caught in a drenching downpour, when merely the thought of drought would have been ludicrous. But heavy rains may be of brief duration; all of August's rain may be concentrated in a couple of days. The water level —which is measured daily by federal officials—may rise steeply, only to fall equally quickly afterward. And it is the level of the water that is critical for the swamp's creatures, and for the life of the swamp itself.

Droughts so extreme that they invite fires of catastrophic dimension seem to occur in the Okefenokee about every 25 to 40 years. Since I had come to know the swamp mostly as a wet world, just the idea of fire seemed a mockery at first. Yet I did not need to be told of the flammability of dried peat, having seen it burned in hearths throughout Ireland. Nor did I need to be convinced that one small spark, taking hold in one parched patch of grass and encouraged by winds, can cause a conflagration that leaps across narrow water barriers. In 1932 a mentally retarded youth, feeling chilled after a day of fishing, tossed a match into such a patch of Okefenokee grass because, he later explained, he wanted to warm his hands. That year the swamp was unusually dry; even the surface muck of the prairies was dry. The fire that followed, driven by high easterly winds, burned out many of the swamp's white bay trees, about 40 to 50 million board feet of its black gums and several million feet of slash pines, and spewed a shower of fiery bits of moss onto the streets of a town a few miles away. "It was a bit like what I imagine hell looks like," Johnny Hickox told me.

The classic arsonist of the Okefenokee, however, is lightning, and there is a classic path that the fires it starts can take. The higher, drier uplands adjoining the swamp, with their dense growths of pines, provide a susceptible starting point. Fire builds up force and heat in these pinelands and moves on to the undergrowth at the fringes of the swamp, destroying shallow-rooted shrubs and young trees. The flames then probe into the interior, reaching the peat. Exposed by drought, the peat burns both on the surface and inside its dried masses, ultimately spreading the flames deep into the vitals of the swamp and to the cypresses, no longer safe in their once-waterlogged bays. A cypress bay may survive fires burning slowly at ground level because cypress foliage is like a topknot on a long stem, giving the tree some protection against fire —unless, driven by high winds, it rushes through the top branches, in a so-called crown fire. Or the fire may burn into the peat around the cypress roots; when this ground support is eaten away by flames, the tree may fall to its death with its trunk and crown still unburned.

The part played by peat in a major conflagration is especially noteworthy. Peat can burn internally for days and even weeks, serving in effect as a reservoir of fire. Even if rain falls the peat may continue to burn until, with the return of dry, windy weather, the fire is reinvigorated. Then, whipped up by a new windstorm, it burns everything in its way—tall tree as well as low bush. It may engulf areas it has previously bypassed, or double back and subject some areas to a second scorching. The burning peat itself may undergo transformation. The peat bed that covers the entire floor of the swamp—except for the islands and deeper lakes—is 5 to 10 feet thick in most places; here and there it is as much as 15 to 20 feet thick. The more severe a drought, the deeper the peat will dry out; the deeper the drying out, the deeper a fire may burn, gouging out "pockets" that markedly alter the look of that part of the Okefenokee. For when the water finally returns to the swamp, these pockets become gator holes or lakes. Or an entire new prairie will result if the upper layer of peat has been burned away deep enough to kill the root systems of all woody growth over an extensive area; the returning water floods the area to a depth that makes it impossible for woody growth to reestablish itself, yet possible for aquatic and marsh vegetation to flourish.

How often in its history the Okefenokee has changed its face in this fundamental way is unknowable. Corings taken throughout the swamp show that there have been many times when the peat has been burned down to a depth of as much as six feet; moreover, charcoal deposits have been found still deeper down, and they are believed to have been left by fires that occurred thousands of years ago.

The large prairies along the eastern side of the swamp—Chase, Chesser, Territory, Grand, Mizell and others—were almost certainly created by fires that swept away centuries of peat build-up. So were at least 40 prairie lakes big enough to merit place names on the map; one of them, the goal of several of my swamp journeys, is Gannet Lake, which covers 27 acres. Some of the lakes may have been formed in relatively modern times, as a result of the so-called Big Fire of 1844, the first of which there is any certain knowledge. No whites had yet settled in the swamp; Dan Lee did not arrive on Billy's Island until nine years later. But Owen Mizell, whose kinfolk were to launch one of the Okefenokee's family dynasties, was then a boy living on the swamp's outskirts. Decades later, Mizell, who went on to become a member of the Georgia state legislature and survived to age 96, remembered that in the fire of 1844 smoke hung over miles of the countryside for several weeks, sometimes in a pall so dense it hid the sun. His elders, Mizell recalled, ever after referred to the event as the time the swamp "burned up," leaving a wasteland of blackened stumps and gaping peat holes.

People living near the swamp today need not hark back that far for spectacular examples of fire's impact on the Okefenokee. Still fresh in local memory are the years 1954 and 1955, when five major fires raged in and around the swamp and burned over almost 360,000 of its acres —about four fifths of its total extent—and 142,000 additional acres of the neighboring uplands. As in the case of the 1844 fire, this holocaust was preceded by a terrible drought. In all of 1954, only 26 inches of rain fell, less than half the annual average for the previous nine years. The water went down so low that large areas of peat were exposed to the Georgia sun, and men could walk on the dried bed of the watercourse north of Billy's Island. Both Minnie's Lake and the fabled Big Water went almost dry. Very little surface water remained anywhere in the swamp, and boat travel became virtually impossible.

Johnny Hickox told me of wandering along the fringes of the swamp that summer and observing the effects of the sparsity of rain on the Okefenokee's multitudes of creatures. Countless fish were trapped in pools that were slowly shrinking to mudholes. As the water fell, each pond became a prime hunting ground for raccoons, otters, opossums, foxes and fish-eating birds. The fish died off in such numbers that the stench of their rotting bodies permeated many parts of the swamp. But the feast did not last long; the feasters themselves eventually became refugees from the drought, seeking food and sanctuary in ever-diminishing water holes or in shallow prairies already overpopulated with resident and immigrant alligators.

For the alligators this was a time of plenty, since many of their customary victims concentrated conveniently at the few watery places that remained. Eventually, however, those hard-pressed mammals and birds that managed to survive simply left the danger areas for greener pastures outside the swamp, and the reptiles and amphibians dug in to wait out the perilous period of feast and famine.

For the greatly reduced fish population, the end of the drought in the summer of 1955 did not bring instant relief—the increased acidity of the low water inhibited their reproduction for several years thereafter. But with the exception of the otters—too many of them ended up inside alligators—the animal population of the swamp was depleted only temporarily. When conditions in the swamp finally returned to normal, its creatures reestablished themselves in their former habitats.

It was still summer in the Okefenokee when the first of the five major fires broke out. In early July, 1954, the 3,000 acres of Billy's Island, consisting mostly of pinewoods, were swept by a ground fire, probably sparked by lightning, that burned for six days. But it could not leap beyond the island's shores because the surrounding peat bed was not yet dry enough to burn.

Five months later, however, the peat everywhere in the swamp was eminently flammable. At the southeastern edge of the Okefenokee a crew of workers who were collecting turpentine lit a campfire to ward off the November chill. The cause of what followed will never be known for sure; the workers disavowed any carelessness and blamed a mule

The cracked earth of a vanished pond (foreground) shows the impact of drought in the Okefenokee in the summer and fall of 1972. The sole hint of the normally watery environment is the coating of green algae under the fallen branches on the parched area, indicating that moisture is still present, possibly from a subterranean spring.

they were using to haul the sleds of turpentine out of the woods. The mule, they said, switched its tail into a bucket of turpentine, then into the campfire; with tail ablaze, it ran into the woods—a living torch setting fires as it went.

In any case, the fire burned west toward the center of the swamp. Then, as now, it was impossible to bring fire-fighting equipment into the swamp. Still, the fire fighters at the fringes thought that the Okefenokee's waters would form a barrier against the flames. In years of normal rainfall and water levels, the Okefenokee does indeed serve this purpose. When a fire occurs in the adjacent higher woodlands in such years, it is standard practice to fight the blaze by "running it into the swamp." But in 1954 conditions in the swamp were far from normal. The peat bed was more than ever receptive to the flames. They moved through the southeastern boglands of the swamp, swung northward, veered again to the east, left the swamp near Chesser Island, and roared into the uplands there. The score of destruction, after nine days of the "Mule-Tail Fire," was more than 33,000 acres of burned swamp and more than 20,000 acres of upland timber almost completely killed.

Meanwhile the western side of the Okefenokee was having its own troubles. In October lightning struck about a mile northeast of Rowell's Island. It started a peat fire that was to smoulder and slowly burn for five months and create such awesome havoc that, perversely, it inspired some unknown arsonist or arsonists. In early March, 1955, a series of incendiary fires were set along a seven-mile stretch between Turkey Branch and Suwannee Creek, a few miles beyond the federal refuge boundaries. These became one big fire that joined the still-burning October fire. This giant conflagration destroyed 318,000 acres of the swamp and 11,000 acres of upland. The fire raged with particular ferocity along the course of the Suwannee River, at one point setting loose an ancient logjam that had impeded the river's free flow into the Gulf of Mexico.

Outside the swamp, much of southeastern Georgia lay under so heavy a blanket of smoke that motorists were forced to drive with their headlights on high beam at midday. The acrid smell of the smoke reached Jacksonville, 40 miles distant down the Atlantic Coast. But it was inside the swamp that the action of the fire was eeriest. For weeks, no flames would be visible; only great pillars of smoke rising from the smouldering peat gave testimony to the presence of fire. Then a wind, or some change in its direction, would send flames leaping high to snatch up the Spanish moss and burn the tall cypresses. Streamers of the burning moss would go spinning off to start new fires elsewhere. In the pinewoods, the fire would sometimes burn sedately at ground level, clearing out undergrowth; then it would be seized by a high wind, roar upward and burn so fiercely into the treetops that thousands of trees died in a few hours.

The Big Fire, as it has come to be called after its namesake of 1844, was not the final catastrophe. Even as it raged, another fire of incendiary origin swept state forest lands at the northern end of the swamp. Unlike the Big Fire, it was brought under control in relatively short order—eight days. But during that time it effected an almost complete kill of timber on about 22,500 upland acres and burned over 5,000 acres of the swamp. The fifth and last fire, in early June, 1955, was set by lightning at the swamp's southwestern edge and destroyed 82,000 acres of pine trees owned by a paper company. In terms of dollars this was the most damaging of all the fires of 1954 and 1955. But their total cost, in noneconomic terms, can never be precisely calculated. When heavy rains put out the last of the flames in the summer of 1955, many areas of the Okefenokee were unrecognizable.

Oldtimers in the Okefenokee used to be philosophic about the havoc caused by fire. They usually lived long enough to see the swamp rise, phoenix-like, from the ashes of its destruction. Under certain conditions they thought fire could be extremely beneficial. Throughout the human history of the swamp, men have set fires in it they could control, in order to gain specific advantages. The Indians seasonally burned sections of forest to flush out the game they hunted. The white settlers on the swamp islands burned certain areas each year to destroy the brush that encroached on the lands they had cleared for cultivation. There were added benefits in the wake of these burnings; the grass that quickly sprang up helped to feed the cattle the settlers were trying to raise, and new undergrowth encouraged the appearance of deer, bringing a favored source of food within easier reach. The practice of controlled burning continues today in the upland pinewoods that border the swamp, carefully supervised by foresters, to remove the accumulations of leaf litter and underbrush that present a fire hazard. The hope is that these small preventive fires will create firebreaks and lessen the risk of a repetition of the holocaust of 1954 and 1955.

A preventive step of a different sort—taken by the federal government after 1955 at the urging of conservationists, forestry officials and owners of land near the Okefenokee—aims at keeping the swamp's water level high enough to prevent a fire from going on an extended rampage. Immense amounts of muck were gouged out with draglines and built up into a sill, or ridge, near where the Suwannee River runs out of the southwestern edge of the swamp. The sill serves as a dam, slowing the flow of water from Billy's Lake, just behind it, and thus also slowing the flow of water from north and east of Billy's Lake. Since the general direction of the swamp's water flow is southwesterly, the sill is strategically situated to ensure that the world of the Okefenokee will remain a wet world, resistant to burning.

But this solution, like all human solutions to wilderness problems, poses a new dilemma. Fire is necessary to clean out the inexorable build-up of peat, layer upon layer, that piles up each year, compacting its rotting generations of dead leaves and grasses so firmly together that other plants and shrubs and trees eventually find foothold there. If this process went on without interruption, the prairies would become densely forested with cypresses, black gums and bays, the boat trails would be filled up and all of the swamp would be woodland.

People who love the Okefenokee as it is shudder at the thought. They confirm the oldtimers' belief that disastrous as fire in the swamp may seem, it also serves as a regenerative force. They find no joy in the sight of prairies, those splendid open stretches of the Okefenokee, reverting to woodland, as some are doing today. By curious happenstance the fires of 1954 and 1955, though they spread far and wide, did not burn deep enough into the swamp's peat bed to create even so much as an acre of new prairie. The Okefenokee's staunchest defenders find this a matter of regret. "Most people thought the fires of 1954 and 1955 were terrible," says Eugene Cypert, a naturalist at the Okefenokee Swamp Park. "But we need another prairie-causing fire; I want to see some prairies restored. I want to see the swamp keep its character."

My last journey in the swamp took me down the Suwannee River below Billy's Lake, a part of the Okefenokee that had become one of my favorite places during my wanderings. The river, at this point, is really a kind of water garden with bands of gorgeous green mosses decorating the bases of the cypresses, the black water meandering along a course that looks as though it had been planned by man. The yellow flowers of some of the water lilies are still in bloom even in early winter; wood ibises and white ibises perch in the trees, immobile, silent, watching. It is a place of great serenity.

On this day a cool wind dimpled the black water and broke the re-

The decayed stump of a burned-out cypress furnishes a fertile bed for sweet pepper bush and swamp fern. Far from being totally disastrous, the fires that occur periodically in times of drought help maintain the balance between swamp, forest, prairie and lake by inhibiting encroaching growth and keeping waterways clear.

flections of the overhanging trees into thousands of dancing, circular distortions. In the middle of the river stood many small mounds, sculpted gracefully upward from the surface of the water—old cypress trunks, so thoroughly colonized by shrubs, ferns and even bay trees that they looked like miniature plant cities. At first I thought these were the trunks of cypresses that had died and fallen, but on closer inspection I saw that they were monuments to the 1954-1955 fire. It had burned so fiercely here that it had reduced the cypresses to the level of the water itself.

As I let my canoe drift, the passing cypress stumps, the silent, watching birds and the decayed wreckage of last summer's plants all somehow seemed to complement my own feelings at leaving the Okefenokee. I had cursed the swamp so often when I had been caught in its clutching fingers that the nostalgia I now felt was like saying goodbye to an old friend with whom I had frequently fought.

The swamp had survived all sorts of tribulations. It had resisted Captain Harry Jackson's efforts to drain it. It had suffered an enormous loss of trees—almost half a billion board feet of pine and cypress, live oak, swamp black gum, red bay, white bay, maple and sweet gum. Its wildlife had been hooked, speared, shot, trapped and skinned in great numbers; in one year when prices of pelts were high, 10,000 raccoons, 200 otters, 50 wildcats, 50 skunks and 2,000 alligators had been dispatched. I did not wish to reduce the Okefenokee to a series of statistics, so contrary to the spirit of the swamp, but somehow the figures of destruction were reassuring because the great morass was still there, and so were most of its animal species.

The swamp had survived repeated plans to drain it and open it to cultivation by means of a canal driven across the top of the Florida peninsula to join the Atlantic and the Gulf of Mexico. It had survived attempts, supported by local counties, chambers of commerce and government agencies, to build a scenic highway through it that would have sent tourists racing along the western side of Big Water, past Minnie's Lake, across Billy's Island and Honey Island.

As dusk grew, I reached the end of the Suwannee's run through the swamp and the site of the five-mile-long earthen sill that had been built after the 1954-1955 fire. Oddly, this massive man-made work, which should have been so alien to the atmosphere of the swamp wilderness, seemed to me to enhance rather than diminish the beauty of the place. Black vultures stood silent along the sill; behind it, on the waters of Billy's Lake, ducks settled like moths.

Sitting in the canoe, I remembered the many earlier times when I had taken temporary leave of the Okefenokee. I left one summer evening when a breathless sun sank behind the great rookery of egrets and herons and ibises on Chesser Prairie; the colors of the sun had fused into the stillness of the waters, and the prairie held luminous silver light in anticipation of night. I left one evening when ibises passed overhead in hundreds, wings rustling like silk being shaken. I left when the full moon was rising, its great white eye appearing through the locked branches of cypress and pine along Sapling Prairie. I left at night from Grand Prairie when alligators surfaced around me, moonlight glistening in their eyes. I left in stifling heat when biting flies and bugs and mosquitoes swarmed around my head. And now I was leaving as a thin, horizontal window of ice lay ahead of my canoe; the previous night had been cold enough to freeze shallow stretches of the Suwannee.

I once asked what use the swamp was to 20th Century man, and in this last leave-taking I had the answer. The Okefenokee is a reminder of man's fallibility in knowing what is best for the earth around him. When his heart is thumping ominously and he is alone, his exertions causing his breath to rasp in his throat, the swamp presents itself boldly as the one true winner against all our notions of a better-ordered earth. In the Okefenokee, man is subdued. The sound of earth overwhelms his voice and tells him that in the long haul he moves to its music. Nature, in the end, simply does not heed man's rules. If that truth is not demonstrable now, then we have lost sight of the meaning of our occupancy of this planet.

A Place of Primitive Beauty

PHOTOGRAPHS BY WOLF VON DEM BUSSCHE

While photographer Wolf von dem Bussche was documenting Billy's Island (pages 86-93), he became so spellbound by the brooding vistas around him that he wandered farther afield in the Okefenokee, traveling through its misty dawns and silent days and translating his feelings into the haunting pictures that follow.

"My purpose on Billy's Island," he said, "was to show the remains of its former colonization by man, to resurrect the past. But it was apparent at once that the power of nature to reclaim its own had almost obliterated all traces of a relatively recent and extensive human presence on the island. This sort of discovery certainly helps to reduce any inflated opinions one might have about man's omnipotence."

As he went deeper into the Okefenokee, von dem Bussche made yet another discovery: all feeling of urgency and dependence on time began to fade as he drifted along the swamp's watercourses. "The entire area is so primitive and sleepy," he said, "that it looks as if someone had stopped the clock. Everything seems so unreal that one begins to think of prehistoric ages."

From first to last, the photographer was particularly enchanted by the serene beauty of this extraordinary world. Seen at close hand, the chaotic growth connoted by the very word swamp sorted itself into a series of distinctive vignettes. Here were the looming silhouettes of cypress trees, the lacelike tracery of Spanish moss and the casual scatter of autumn leaves. As his boat moved slowly through the tangle of aquatic plants, von dem Bussche could not fail to be impressed by the black and bottomless look of the water around him, an effect created by the dark peat below it. The water provided a perfect mirror to reflect the ever-changing scenery along the banks.

With the photographer's eye that is forever alert to the quality of the light that bathes his subject, von dem Bussche found the Okefenokee a photographer's dream. As he described it: "Early in the morning, right after sunrise, there was a dense fog that made everything seem covered with cobwebs, as if overnight a very fine net had been dropped over the landscape. By noon, the sun had burned off the fog and the light was brilliant everywhere, but it mellowed perceptibly as the day wore on. When night fell, everything became so black and so scary that it was a relief to get out."

CYPRESS TREES AT DAWN, TINSELED WITH SPANISH MOSS

POND LILIES AND MAIDEN-CANE GRASS, SPOTLIGHTED BY THE SUN

DEBRIS-DRAPED CASSENA HOLLY AND ITS WATERY IMAGE

WATER-SWEPT SPIKE RUSH

WHITE BILLOWS OF PERENNIAL FENNEL IN BLOOM

BASE OF A CYPRESS MIRRORED IN A POND

SWAMP PLANTS AND CYPRESS LOGS

BLACK GUMS ALONG THE SHORE OF BILLY'S ISLAND

Bibliography

Bland, John H., *Forests of Lilliput: The Realm of Mosses and Lichens.* Prentice-Hall, Inc., 1971.

Brockman, C. Frank, *Trees of North America.* Western Publishing Company, 1968.

Burt, William H., *A Field Guide to the Mammals.* Houghton Mifflin Company, 1976.

Cobb, Boughton, *A Field Guide to the Ferns and Their Related Families.* Houghton Mifflin Company, 1977.

Collingwood, G. H., and Warren D. Brush, *Knowing Your Trees.* The American Forestry Association, 1964.

Conant, Roger, *A Field Guide to Reptiles and Amphibians of Eastern and Central North America.* Houghton Mifflin Company, 1975.

Cruickshank, Helen Gere, ed., *John and William Bartram's America.* Devin, 1981.

Dana, Mrs. William Starr, *How to Know the Wild Flowers.* Dover Publications, Inc., 1963.

Ewan, Joseph, ed., *William Bartram Botanical and Zoological Drawings, 1756-1788.* The American Philosophical Society, 1968.

Georgia Guide, Work Projects Administration. University of Georgia Press, 1940.

Harrar, Ellwood S. and J. George, *Guide to Southern Trees.* Dover Publications, Inc., 1962.

Johnson, James R., *The Southern Swamps of America.* David McKay Company, Inc., 1970.

Lloyd, Francis Ernest, *The Carnivorous Plants.* Dover Publications, Inc., 1976.

Longstreet, R. J., ed., *Birds of Florida.* Trend Publications, 1965.

McQueen, A. S., and Hamp Mizell, *History of Okefenokee Swamp.* Press of Jacobs and Company, 1926.

Matschat, Cecile Hulse, *Suwannee River: Strange Green Land.* Brown Thrasher Books, 1980.

Oliver, James A., *The Natural History of North American Amphibians and Reptiles.* D. Van Nostrand Company, Inc., 1955.

Peck, Robert, ed., *Travels of William Bartram.* Peregrine Smith, 1980.

Peterson, Roger Tory, *A Field Guide to the Birds.* Houghton Mifflin Company, 1980.

Petrides, George A., *A Field Guide to Trees and Shrubs.* Houghton Mifflin Company, 1973.

Pope, Clifford H., *The Reptile World.* Alfred A. Knopf, 1955.

Rand, Austin L., *Birds of North America.* Doubleday & Company, 1971.

Rickett, Harold William, *Wild Flowers of the United States: The Southern States,* 2 vols. McGraw-Hill Book Company, 1967.

Robbins, Chandler S., Bertel Bruun and Herbert S. Zim, *Birds of North America: A Guide to Field Identification.* Western Publishing Company, 1966.

Silvics of Forest Trees of the United States. U.S. Department of Agriculture, Forest Service, 1965.

Wright, Albert Hazen, *Life-Histories of the Frogs of Okefenokee Swamp, Georgia.* The Macmillan Company, 1932.

Young, Stanley P., *The Bobcat of North America.* University of Nebraska Press, 1978.

Periodicals, Articles and Pamphlets

Coulter, E. Merton, "The Okefenokee Swamp, Its History and Legends, Part I." *Georgia Historical Quarterly,* vol. XLVIII (June 1964), pp. 166-189.

Cypert, Eugene, "The Effects of Fire in the Okefenokee Swamp in 1954 and 1955." *The American Midland Naturalist,* vol. 66 (October 1961), pp. 485-503.

Cypert, Eugene, "The Origin of Houses in the Okefenokee Prairies." *The American Midland Naturalist,* vol. 87 (April 1972), pp. 448-458.

Cypert, Eugene, *Plant Succession on Burned Areas in Okefenokee Swamp Following the Fires of 1954 and 1955.* Tall Timbers Fire Ecology Conference, Proceedings, no. 12 (1973), Tallahassee, Florida.

Elkins, Liston, *Story of the Okefenokee.* Okefenokee Swamp Park, 1967.

Harper, Francis, "The Mammals of the Okefenokee Swamp Region of Georgia." *Boston Society of Natural History,* vol. 38 (March 1927), pp. 193-396.

Izlar, Robert Lee, *The Hebard Lumber Company in the Okefenokee Swamp: Thirty-Six Years of Southern Logging History.* Unpublished M.S. thesis, University of Georgia, 1971.

Macneil, F. Stearns, *Pleistocene Shore Lines in Florida and Georgia.* U.S. Geological Survey, Professional Paper 221-F, 1950.

Mattoon, Wilbur R., *The Southern Cypress.* U.S. Dept. of Agriculture Bulletin 272, September 1915.

Smedley, Jack E., *Summary Report on the Geology and Mineral Resources of the Okefenokee National Wildlife Refuge, Georgia.* U.S. Geological Survey Bulletin 1260-N, 1968.

Wright, Albert H., and S. W. Funkhouser, *A Biological Reconnaissance of the Okefenokee Swamp in Georgia: The Reptiles.* Proceedings of the Academy of Natural Sciences of Philadelphia, vol. LXVII (March 1915), pp. 107-192.

Wright, Albert H., and Francis Harper, "A Biological Reconnaissance of Okefenokee Swamp: The Birds." *The Auk: A Quarterly Journal of Ornithology,* vol. XXX (October 1913), pp. 477-505.

Wright, Albert H., and A. A. Wright, "The Habitats and Composition of the Vegetation of Okefenokee Swamp, Georgia." *Ecological Monographs,* vol. II (April 1932), pp. 110-232.

Acknowledgments

The author and editors of this book wish to thank the following persons and institutions: E. Ross Allen, Ross Allen's Reptile Institute, Silver Springs, Fla.; Atlanta Archives, Central Research Department, Atlanta, Ga.; Donald F. Bruning, Asst. Curator of Ornithology, New York Zoological Park, N.Y.C.; Cornell University, John M. Olin Research Library, Ithaca, N.Y.; Eugene Cypert, Naturalist, Okefenokee Swamp Park, Waycross, Ga.; Joseph A. Davis, Scientific Assistant to the Director, New York Zoological Park, N.Y.C.; Wilbur H. Duncan, Professor of Botany, University of Georgia, Athens; John R. Eadie, Manager, Okefenokee National Wildlife Refuge, Waycross, Ga.; Richard Eichhorn, Division of Refuge Management, Fish and Wildlife Service, Washington, D.C.; Liston Elkins, Waycross, Ga.; John Hickox, Chief Guide, Okefenokee Swamp Park, Waycross, Ga.; Sidney S. Horenstein, Department of Invertebrate Paleontology, The American Museum of Natural History, N.Y.C.; Beverly Kokinos, Flemington, N.J.; O. Gordon Langdon, Research Project Leader, U.S. Forest Service, Southeastern Forest Experiment Station, Charleston, S.C.; Terry Lindsay, Okefenokee National Wildlife Refuge, Waycross, Ga.; Wendell D. Metzen, Refuge Biologist, Okefenokee National Wildlife Refuge, Waycross, Ga.; Larry G. Pardue, New York Botanical Garden, N.Y.C.; Jacqueline Russell, Frenchtown, N.J.; Zack Seymour, Supervisor, Dixon Memorial State Forest, Waycross, Ga.; Jack Stubbs, Principal Silviculturist, U.S. Forest Service, Southeastern Forest Experiment Station, Charleston, S.C.; Jimmy Walker, Manager, Okefenokee Swamp Park, Waycross, Ga.; Janina Weiner, American Museum of Natural History, N.Y.C.; Richard G. Zweifel, Chairman and Curator, Department of Herpetology, American Museum of Natural History, N.Y.C.

Picture Credits

Sources for the pictures in this book are shown below. Credits for pictures from top to bottom are separated by dashes; from left to right they are separated by commas.

The cover and all photographs by Patricia Caulfield except: Front end papers 2, 3—Wendell D. Metzen. Front end paper 4, page 1—Ron Sherman. 2, 3—Edwin B. Fortson Jr. 8, 9—Robert Walch. 10, 11—William J. Bolte. 18, 19—Map by R. R. Donnelley Cartographic Services. 22—Drawing by Vincent Lewis. 45—Trustees of The British Museum (Natural History). 46 —Jack Dermid. 49—Bottom left Jack Dermid. 63—Right center D. W. Pfitzer. 64—Left E. Yaw—Jack Dermid. 70 —Courtesy of Moneta Hewett. 74— A. H. Wright Collection courtesy Cornell University. 78, 79—A. H. Wright Collection courtesy Cornell University. 82, 83—Courtesy of Moneta Hewett. 87 through 93—Wolf von dem Bussche. 96—Leonard Lee Rue III. 103—William J. Bolte. 109—James P. Valentine. 112, 113—Wendell D. Metzen. 117—Lower left George A. Elbert, lower right Grant Heilman. 122, 123—Right Wendell D. Metzen. 128, 129—Edwin B. Fortson Jr. 138, 139—Edwin B. Fortson Jr. 146 through 155—Robert Walch. 169 through 179—Wolf von dem Bussche.

Index

*Numerals in italics indicate a
photograph or drawing of the subject
mentioned.*